WRITING FOR THE TEENAGE MARKET

WRITING FOR THE TEENAGE MARKET

Ann de Gale

A & C Black · London

First published 1993
A & C Black (Publishers) Limited
35 Bedford Row, London WC1R 4JH

ISBN 0–7136–3788–9

A CIP catalogue record for this book is available from the British Library

Cover illustration by Conny Jude

Typeset in 11/12 pt Palatino by Florencetype Ltd, Kewstoke, Avon
Printed in Great Britain by Biddles Ltd, Guildford, Surrey

Contents

Acknowledgements

I wish to thank everyone who has helped me with the preparation of this book, in and out of working hours. These people, and many more, have provided information, opinions and introductions to writers and readers, and also books, catalogues and editorial guidelines. I am also deeply grateful to all those who granted me interviews and permission to quote extracts from their books and other written works.

Writers: Annie Dalton, Julian Flood, Shirley Harrison, Mary Hooper, Kenneth Ireland, Pete Johnson, Alison Legh-Jones, Christine Pullein-Thompson, Lorna Read and Jean Ure.

Publishing directors and editors: Peter Day (Allison & Busby), Vix Eldon and Susie Gibbs (Pan Macmillan), Miriam Hodgson (Methuen), Jane Nissen (Hamish Hamilton), Amanda Smith (Samuel French).

Playwrights: Roy Apps, Sally Worboyes (Fen Farm) and Polly Thomas (New Playwrights' Trust).

Literary agents: Jennifer Luithlen and Maggie Noach.

From the Book Trust's Children's Book Foundation: Lindsey Fraser and Ann Sohn-Rethel. From the Lancashire County Library: David Lightfoot and others concerned with the Children's Book of the Year publications. From Chiswick: librarian Helen O'Brien and staff at the Fountain bookshop.

From Forest School, Snaresbook: Andrew Boggis (Warden), Gerald Wright (English Department) and eight friendly pupils.

Finally, barrister, Peter Mason, who helped to put me on the right side of the law.

For Simon and Sam, Jo and Jenny, Nick and Emma, with apologies for neglecting them while writing this book.

Introduction

In this book, along with the whys and wherefores, I hope to pass on some of the excitement I feel about writing for young adults. Call them teenagers, older children or what you will, but the important point is that they have reached an age when they choose much of their reading matter for themselves. Adults still have their influence, but parents hold far less of the power they rightly enjoyed when buying, say, a boxed set of Beatrix Potter books for a four-year-old. Teachers, anxious to instil a love of books, recognize their older pupils' need to experiment, to compare one author with another and discuss their preferences in and out of the classroom. Nowadays, school set books often include popular modern fiction along with classical literature, and it is more or less accepted that lightweight romances and teen magazines play their part in encouraging young people to read. Publishers, with an eye on sales figures, seek out and value the opinions of children old enough to be seen *and* heard.

However much I enjoy writing for the very young, I feel that with teenagers I have the added interest of a much more direct approach. Of course it pays to give some thought to adults lurking in the background, and the secret here, perhaps, is to be aware, but not restrictingly wary.

The aims of this book

First of all, I want to stress that this is not a how-to-write manual. Writing is a very personal business. Methods and work patterns vary, sometimes astonishingly, from author to author and there is no standard, expertly signposted route to success. This book is for writers, new or established, keen to learn more about the craft and technique of writing for older children. The opportunities explored range from novels, short stories, plays and non-fiction books to magazine features, serials and picture stories.

The basic necessities are an ability to write readable material, a genuine interest in young people and a shrug-the-shoulders willingness to persevere, because disappointments are inevitable. Luck plays its part, as it does in just about everything, and a sense of humour helps in more ways than you might at first suspect. Some writers seem able to hide acutely sensitive personalities beneath impenetrably thick skins. I don't know how they manage this, but I envy them.

Writers are notorious rule-breakers, but most professionals agree on the importance of studying the rules of the trade before deciding upon which to follow and which to by-pass. It would be foolish, for example, for a beginner to ignore all standard advice on correct presentation; it is hard enough to impress publishers and editors without lumbering them with lengthy manuscripts in single-space typing. Rules such as this are not petty, there are sound reasons for most of them, but we'll go into the practicalities at a later stage.

In order to give as broad a picture as possible of the openings in this market, I have enlisted the help of a number of experienced writers: novelists and other story-tellers, playwrights, non-fiction experts and magazine journalists. Publishers have also had their say, along with librarians, a laywer, booksellers, teachers and, of course, the young readers themselves (including the 10, 11 and 12-year-old devotees of so-called 'teenage' books, journals and drama.)

Of all the comments and suggestions made to me, two stand out from the rest, not merely because I agree with them wholeheartedly, but also because I have heard them over and over again.

- Read and keep on reading the work of successful writers in the field which interests you most – not to imitate their style or filch their plots, but to assess why their writings are so popular with young people.
- Meet and talk to teenagers whenever you can, on their own ground, if possible. Listen to the way they talk and their views on parents, teachers, politicians, old people, friends, books, crime, TV, royalty – everything.

Snippets of wisdom like this are, of course, a roundabout

way of saying *study the market*. And although authors and their readers play major roles in this book, it seems sensible to pay them a little preliminary attention, by way of setting the scene and helping new writers to feel part of it. Let's start with the readers, giving them the priority they rightly deserve.

The readers

These young people provide much of the excitement I mentioned earlier, and they also bring some of the challenge which spurs writers on to put pens to paper and to keep them there, ignoring a million and one other intrusions into their lives. It's a mistake to try to categorize the readers, because there is surely no such thing as a typical teenager. There are goodies and baddies, sparklers and bores, the ones who'll welcome a birthday present microscope and the others who'll throw it at the nearest cat. It is their age which groups them together in a book like this, and the simple way of quelling pie-in-the-sky hopes of pleasing them all is by concentrating on interesting as many of them as possible, within your own field.

Nobody needs to be told that some adolescents grow up faster than others, but it pays to think through the reasons for this, which may have little to do with basic intelligence. Their reading preferences are not easy to analyse. A fifteen-year-old, studying Shakespeare and Jane Austen for exams and impressing teachers with her interest in literature old and new, will quite likely find the need to relax, now and again, with a pile of raunchy magazines. This is quite normal – and why shouldn't teenagers be fascinated by sex? Not only have they to contend with disturbing bodily changes, but as often as not it's the main topic of conversation among the adults all around them, on and off the screen.

It is also worth considering that young people have tremendous demands made on their time: school, friends, sport, music, romance and Television with a capital T. It's hardly surprising that so many of them have to be lured and cajoled by caring adults, skilful writers included, into a love of books. Recently my grown-up up daughter interrupted a conversation, saying, 'I wish you lot would stop knocking Enid Blyton. It was through her I discovered the *fun* of reading books.'

Older people who talk indignantly of the decadence of modern-day youth, lack of discipline and so on, seem to forget that these so-called tearaways are approaching adulthood in a world which is changing too fast for anyone's comfort and where nothing can be taken for granted any more. It's not so much a matter of crazy mixed-up kids, but more a case of hopelessly mixed-up everyone. Of course young people are confused and of course many of them rebel, deciding that a live-for-today policy is the safest way through.

Talk to them and you'll discover that on the whole they feel they've been children for long enough. 10 and 11-year-olds are impatient to be teenagers – the next step towards adulthood – and publishers have to be highly aware of this. When giving a 'Teens' or 'Young Adult' logo to a collection of paperbacks, say, they know and cater for the fact that many, or even most, books in the series will be of particular interest to slightly younger readers. 14-year-olds may still enjoy them in private, but usually prefer to be seen reading adult books and tend to dismiss any such labelling as kids' stuff – and therefore part of their past. This is why many writers – sensibly thinking of sales – aim their work at the younger end of the market.

Like everyone else I know, teenagers hate being talked down to. Understandably, they expect to be given reasons for any advice offered, and some demand sounder reasons than others. They are people, remember, likable and otherwise, but always personalities in their own right. They may be friendly and fun – or wary and insolent. Just because you write for them, you don't have to claim to love them all. How could they respect you if you did?

The writers

There are two frequently aired misconceptions which I'm anxious to scotch right from the start. The first is that all writers for this market are either parents or teachers of teenage children. The simple truth is that some are and some are not, although many of the authors I met while preparing this book had taught in schools at one time or another.

Of course it helps to live or work with young people, but there are countless other ways of getting to know them, to talk and absorb their jargon. (I'll be discussing jargon later, but rest assured – it's not the horrendous hurdle many beginner-writers think it is.)

In my time, I have helped with school swimming sessions and excursions, played the part of prompter to an under-eighteens drama group and acted as courier's mate-cum-dogsbody on an organized holiday for over-twelves. Even when my own kids were the right age, I sometimes found that friends' children were of more practical value, showing a far keener interest in my characters and plots. To them I was a novelty, not just someone who was forever hunched over her typewriter, callously ignoring the hungry mouths crying out to be fed.

Award-winning novelist, Jean Ure, has written over fifty books for young people, but is neither a parent nor a teacher. Lorna Read, editor of the 'young adult' magazine, *Loving*, has no children of her own, but is the author of several novels and hundreds of short stories and articles for teenagers. Pete Johnson, who gave up teaching to become a full-time novelist, has gathered together a panel of young readers who vet and comment on his work before he lets it anywhere near his publisher's desk. Talks with these and many other writers have strengthened my theory that older children often speak more freely to people outside their immediate, everyday circle.

The second myth is far more irritating and crops up regularly, defying all attempts to crush it ruthlessly underfoot. It concerns the assumption that people who write for teenagers are bravely and reluctantly settling for second best after failing in their efforts to break into the adult market. This is a ridiculous attitude, but it can be a hurtful one, which is the only reason I'm bothering to mention it now.

Scan the 'young adult' shelves in a public library and you will almost certainly find novels written specifically for teenagers by authors equally or even more well known for their books for grown-ups. One example is Anne Fine, writer of *Goggle-eyes* and also the acclaimed adult novel, *Taking the Devil's Advice*. Librarians report that Roald Dahl's books are in constant demand by children of all ages, and yet his short stories for adults earned him the enviable title of 'absolute master of twist-in-the-tale'. Perhaps the most convincing argument in favour of stamping out the myth was put forward by Alan Garner whose novel, *The Owl Service*, won him both the Carnegie Medal and *The Guardian* prize for the best book for young people of its year. Talking about the teenage novel, he said, 'It's not a minor form . . . it's a superb discipline which makes me write a better book.'

Not many people survive by writing alone and even fewer can afford to write to please themselves all the time. When I was made redundant from my full-time editorial job four years ago, I began working on an adult novel and a radio play, keeping myself alive (and surprisingly happy) by writing photostory serials and magazine fiction and features. Friendships with other writers in the same situation became closer as we compared notes and swapped news of possible openings. We were all trying to fit in time for more serious projects, but the comparatively quick financial return of 'bread-and-butter' work considerably eased the strain.

I talked to several writers about the problems of tackling a deadlined book while doing a full-time, salaried job, and none of them had found the pressure unbearable. 'Yes, it was exhausting,' said Sally Sheringham, whose entertaining novel, *Cuckoo in the Nest*, has been praised by both adult and older teenage readers, 'but it was the sheer excitement which kept me going.' I remember this feeling well myself: setting the alarm for five-thirty a.m., racing home from work and experiencing none of the usual guilt when buying yet another carton of ready-cooked lasagne from the Italian place on the corner. Leisure activities had to be cut to a drastic minimum of course, but at least I was able to use 'the book' as a convenient excuse for turning down unpleasing invitations.

If, as I claimed earlier, there is no such thing as a typical teenager, the same must be said about the people who write for them. Many stick to rigid rules, starting each day on the dot of nine, some will only write when their children are at school or their spouses at work, while others find themselves horribly frustrated by any kind of discipline and will write for twenty hours one day and twenty minutes the next. I have friends in the trade who shudder at the very mention of writers' circles, but know many people who find them immensely valuable. Apart from the skill of 'readability', there seems to be just one quality shared by all successful writers for young adults, and this is the faculty of remembering quite clearly, and in considerable detail, how they thought and felt as teenagers themselves. When I put this view to author Mary Hooper, she smiled and took it one stage further. 'At times I feel convinced I'm immature,' she said, 'and I'm quite certain this has helped me more than anything when writing for kids.'

Mary's teenage novels have sold all over the world, so it seems that immaturity may not be such a bad thing after all. At times.

1
The novel: preparing the way

Although the first part of this book is concerned mainly with the craft of writing novels for young adults, I hope it will be of interest and practical help, here and there, to writers and would-be writers keen to break into other branches of the teenage market.

Novelists are story-tellers and most of them told stories to themselves, and anybody else willing to listen, long before they'd even heard the word 'novel'. Creating characters, and the adventures which befell them, was an intrinsic part of their childhood, an absorbing way of passing the time and amusing themselves while recovering from chickenpox or waiting for the rain to stop. Gradually and probably reluctantly, they learned to distinguish between innocent story-telling and deliberate lying but I, for one, found it hard to accept the hackneyed presumption that fact was stranger than fiction.

Sometimes, the children who tell stories for fun grow up into adults who, sooner or later, think in terms of writing fiction for money. Their age when embarking upon a novel for readers of any age is of little importance, and Mary Wesley and Patricia Angadi are living proof of this. Jean Ure wrote the first of over fifty published books for young adults while she was still at school, but there are many established writers who didn't turn their attention to the teenage market until they were well over forty. On the whole, I'd prefer to ignore the question of age and concentrate on the more relevant problem of how to get started in the first place.

Try not to to be daunted by gloom merchants who tell you that teenage books are out of favour these days. True, there is far less interest in simple boy-girl romances than there was in the 1980s, but publishers are still on the lookout for new ideas and original treatment. When I discussed this with Victoria Eldon, senior commissioning editor at Pan Macmillan, she stressed the need for try-and-try again optimism, saying, 'If something is good it stands a fair chance, eventually, of getting through.' She added that there were convincing signs of a healthier demand, in the very near future, for teenage novels – and Miriam Hodgson, editorial director of Methuen Children's Books, supported this encouraging forecast.

I've already given a few reasons for studying the market, and now here's another. When reading and mulling over other people's work, you'll quite possibly feel uncontrollably impatient to begin something of your own. This ploy seems to work for me, whenever I'm planning a new writing project. From time to time I come across a book which, in my opinion, is very bad indeed, and I think smugly that I could do far better myself. But then a taunting little voice inside me says, 'Why *don't* you, then?'

While devising a plot and creating characters of your own, you'll almost certainly derive tremendous benefit from examining successful novels by established authors in this genre, comparing the popular easy-reads with the more demanding books, and new favourites with old. This is the writers' equivalent of shopping around and helps them to assess their own capabilities by discovering books of a kind they might feel happy and able (more or less) to tackle themselves. The names of possible publishers can be jotted down for future reference, and of course it makes sense to use public libraries for this sort of research, for reasons of economy, obviously, and also because most junior section librarians seem to enjoy talking about the books on their shelves and have first-hand experience of readers' preferences. It pays to choose off-peak times, the earlier in the day, the better, I've found.

(I suggest you buy, rather than borrow, an up-to-date copy of either the *Writers' and Artists' Yearbook* (A & C Black) or *The Writer's Handbook* (Macmillan). In these you will find not only the addresses and interests of publishers in the United Kingdom and elsewhere, but also details of other markets and a fund of essential information for new and established authors.)

Teenage novels – then and now

Until the 1960s, very few books were written specifically for adolescents. Before then, most children progressed from, say, C.S.Lewis, Malcolm Savile, Arthur Ransome and school stories (with titles like *No Peace for the Prefects*) to J.D. Salinger (*The Catcher in the Rye*), Denis Wheatley and, perhaps, Monica Dickens and Ursula Bloom. The more scholarly enjoyed *Jane Eyre* and *Pride and Prejudice*, as they still do, and soon showed an ecclectic interest in the adult literature of the time.

Way back in the late 1940s, I seem to remember I was in the process of deserting Agatha Christie for D.H. Lawrence and the brothers Waugh, when a fellow sixth former lent me *Seventeenth Summer*, a simple story of first love by Irish-American writer, Maureen Daly. I devoured it at one sitting because, however mawkish this may sound, I had never before come across a book which seemed to be directed at the likes of *me*, with a schoolgirl heroine tussling with parental disapproval of 'dating', while she waited in suspense for the phone to ring with an invitation to the dance. What surprises me now is that this was the *only* novel of its kind which came my way and, although it's still talked about by modern-day children's book specialists, I suspect that sheer novelty value was at least part of the reason for its popularity, all those years ago, with me and my contemporaries.

It wasn't until the 1960s that teenage fiction came into its own, and Alan Garner and American, one-time teacher, Paul Zindel, were among the highly respected authors responsible for this breakthrough. While not attaining the cult-like renown of Tolkien's *Lord of the Rings* trilogy, Garner's books were, and still are, read and acclaimed by adults as well as older children. After the success of *The Owl Service*, countless other writers adopted his technique of interweaving fantasy, myth and folklore with twentieth-century reality, and the demand by young adults for tales of the supernatural grew rapidly. Today, to the alarm of some parents and teachers, teenage horror stories have become very big business indeed.

Paul Zindel's novels, written with zany wit and Pied-Piper-like charm, have been attracting young readers for nearly thirty years. Of *The Pigman*, his first and most famous, educationalist, Aidan Chambers, wrote 'The story is original, and the writing inventive, fast-moving and convincingly contemporary.' Understandably enough, books pinpointing the problems of communication between adults and adolescents are still very much in vogue, but it is, I think, Zindel's inimitable blend of humour and compassion which puts his novels in a class of their own.

For better or for worse, the 1970s brought Judy Blume and the dramatic rise of the teenage love story, which spread through the Eighties and continues to thrive today. Blume has many scathing critics, but her books are phenomenally successful, probably because of her uncompromising handling of the problems of puberty, physical and emotional. While I'm not suggesting a cover-to-cover, in-depth study of any of her novels, I think it would be foolish for a would-be writer of teenage fiction to ignore her work altogether. There's one *non*-fiction book which might possibly be of inspirational benefit: *Letters to Judy*. In this she plays agony aunt to a selection of the young readers (mostly, but not all, girls) who have supposedly written to her about the trials of adolescence. One reviewer recommended the book to perplexed parents, but I feel it might be of equal value to would-be writers of teenager fiction, struggling with the complexities of plotting and characterisation. Don't be put off by the somewhat aggressively American flavour; Blume has cornered a sizable chunk of the British market and it makes good sense to ponder over the reasons for her success.

Finding a slot in today's market

I asked several junior section librarians about the more popular novels for 11-to-14-year-olds and every one of them remarked on the best-selling 'Sweet Valley High' series of paperbacks: stories of boy-girl entanglements at an American coeducational school. There are dozens and dozens of them – *Wrong Kind of Girl* and *Forbidden Love* are just two of the titles – and, to meet the staggering demand, the original author, Francine Pascal, has now been joined by other named writers.

'Sweet Dreams', another highly popular series imported from the States, has also won the hearts of British schoolgirls and, after various attempts in the Seventies and Eighties, most publishers in this country have, for the time being at any rate, stopped trying to compete with the American puppy-love market. When I suggested to Victoria Eldon at Pan Macmillan that Californian beaches probably provided a more romantic setting for experimental kisses, she reminded me that the teenage book industry was a far more formidable force in America, where formula-writing flourished and publishers were known to provide writers not merely with editorial assistance, but often with carefully prepared themes and story-lines as well.

To many of us it is not a particularly sad fact that there is little scope nowadays on this side of the Atlantic for stories based wholly on the intricacies of boy-girl relationships. (The situation may change, of course, as it so often does, and there may well be openings for British writers in the new series of Scholastic Hippo Books – 'Point of Romance' – now at an experimental stage.)

Romance still plays it part, very much so, in many successful novels for teenagers and even younger readers, but publishers are looking for other ingredients, too. It is no longer the accepted norm for young lovers-to-be to 'bump into each other' at a disco or party, and first meetings are more likely to occur by way of a shared interest, project or predicament: investigating rumours of eerie goings-on in a derelict building, maybe, plotting a campaign to save a patch of woodland from destruction by property developers – or waiting in the dole queue, even. It has been suggested that Joan Lingard's *The Twelfth of July* made frequent appearances on secondary school set-book lists partly because of its concern with events in Northern Ireland.

I think it's unlikely that people who scoff at teenage romance – and I've met quite a few in my time – have bothered to read Michelle Magorian's *A Little Love Song*. This novel, set in 1943, is the story of a 17-year-old girl who contrasts her own experiences of first love with those of a young diarist at the beginning of the twentieth century. The familiar themes of family rivalry and youth and war have been given refreshingly new, but gently sensitive treatment and I particularly admired the author's uncompromising honesty when portraying the fumbling awkwardness which so often dims the excitement of early sexual encounters and the dire consequences, eighty or even fifty years ago, of being young, unmarried and pregnant. The only similarity I can find between this book and the American high school romance lying beside it on my table is the publication date of 1991.

The emotional turmoil of teenage pregnancy has also been tackled with great sympathy by Berlie Doherty in her award-winning book, *Dear Nobody*. Readers' appreciation of this and other thought-provoking love stories proves that by no means do all young adults wish to be protected, in romantic fiction, from the crueller facts of life.

I mentioned earlier the extraordinary craze for horror stories which hit the popular market early this decade with the 'Point Horror' paperback series (Scholastic Hippo Books). Depressingly, I have to say that this seems to be another case of 'America rules, OK', but would-be writers of easy-read teenage horror novels (oh dear) may be consoled by the news of possible openings for British writers in the new Red Fox series targeted at readers with a taste for terror in a modern-day setting. Several novels in this series by American, Jesse Harris, have already been published under the collective title of *The Power*, and revolve round the hair-raising experiences of McKenzie Gold, the schoolgirl protagonist who, according to one of the blurbs, is 'smart, pretty – and she's psychic.' Death and suicide seem to be part of this child's everyday concern, and it is hardly surprising that the blurb promoting her 'power' goes on to ask, '*. . . is it a gift or a curse?*'

I would hate to show sneering disapproval of these or any other series of undemanding novels for younger teenagers, and it would be both condescending and hypocritical of me to do so. As Lindsey Fraser, Director, Book Trust Scotland pointed out, they fill a need by interesting kids in books, and often pave the way for more serious reading. People exploring the possibilities of survival by writing alone, sometimes find they have a talent for writing for the highly popular but perhaps less literary end of the market – and go on to achieve great enjoyment from making a comfortable living this way. Many new writers give first priority to getting work published – as proof of their abilities – and decide to change direction later on. (Some may be interested to hear that the publishers of Scholastic Hippo Books are considering the work of British authors while preparing two more teenage series: 'Point Fantasy' and 'Point Crime'.)

Young readers are clearly fascinated by tales of fantasy and the supernatural (science fiction included) and these do *not* have to be horror stories – but thrillers of all kinds are in demand and so are books with a sporting or career background. While some writers prefer to concentrate on a subject with which they are already familiar, others happily explore new ground, looking upon research as not so much a chore, but more a fascinating part of their work.

If, on the other hand, you are considering a deeply controversial or disturbingly emotional theme, you'll probably find that no amount of reading and research can make up for a total lack of first-hand experience. As an obvious example, novelists who, as children, suffered the pain and devastation of parental divorce have a head start – though not a particularly enviable one – when writing about the troubled young victims of broken homes.

Few people have the courage and dedication of Robert Swindells who, while planning his thriller, *Stone Cold*, concerning the plight of homeless young adults, spent three nights living rough on the streets of London.

I was going through a truly awful tug-of-love situation when I wrote the first of my own three novels for teenagers. I'd resisted the temptation to sell an article – along the lines of 'I kidnapped my own son' – to one of the more sensational magazines of the early Eighties, but was able to compare my own feelings with those of that same son, when writing the book, which was based on our shared experience of a holiday for single parents and their children in Corfu. The two main characters were imaginary, but the emotional implications and the humour of the somewhat zany setting were there for the taking.

Pete Johnson talked to me of the empathy he felt with Caro, the girl in his ghost story, *We the Haunted*, who found it impossible to face up to the reality of her boyfriend's death. 'My father died from a sudden heart attack when I was fifteen,' Pete explained, 'and although I dissuaded my mother from seeing a medium, I eventually visited a spiritualist myself, with one of my father's possessions. These experiences helped me, I think, to write convincingly of Caro's thoughts and doubts about the finality of bereavement.'

When we went on to discuss his policy of writing to interest readers of both sexes, I pointed out that many people, including those who should know better, assumed that teenage novels were only read by girls. Pete replied that he received as many letters from boys as he did from girls with worries about relationships and that he was occasionally asked why the young guys in some books seemed to be there solely as objects of desire, pity or scorn, and often came across as characterless and virtually brain-dead.

Now we are moving back to the all-important question of

how to please the readers, and I have permission to include a few extracts from reviews written by older schoolchildren when playing their part in selecting the winners of the annual Lancashire County Library/National Westminster Bank Children's Book of the Year Award. For this contest, publishers throughout the country are invited each year to nominate books from their lists, and these are read and judged by a panel of 13-14-year-old pupils from Lancashire secondary schools.

I have chosen one winning novel and six which were short-listed for the award over the last three years, hoping the comments will help new writers in their exploration of themes and plots of current interest – particularly as the young reviewers took care to explain *why* they were recommending the books.

Plague 99 by Jean Ure (Methuen) – Winner, 1990.
Plague 99 is a book set 9 years into the future. . . Fran arrived home to find a letter saying that her parents were dead upstairs. The book did bring tears to my eyes because it made you think about death, it made you think that the same thing could happen to you . . . the title made you want to read to find out what the plague was . . . it is suitable for both sexes and the right age group. . .
Debbie Smith

Ghost Abbey by Robert Westall (Macmillan) – Shortlisted, 1990
. . . Maggi's father is offered a job, working on an old house . . . Maggi can sense danger . . . a helper is paralysed when he brings damage to the house . . . Maggi finally sees a pattern, and she knows the family has to leave. What does the house want with them? And will they live long enough to leave? I really enjoyed this book, it had an air of mystery to it, as well as involving you until the end. . .
Sarah Blackburn

Penalty by Michael Hardcastle (Dent) – Shortlisted, 1991
. . . It was brilliant . . . one of those books that if you pick it up it is a struggle to put down . . . gripping stuff for everyone from the age of 11 to 14.'
C.W.

Kiss the Dust by Elizabeth Laird (Heinemann) Runner-up, 1992
. . . It is about a family of Kurds from Iraq who flee over the mountains to Iran. . . The story is based on the young girl called Tara mostly as she goes through all the changes in life as a refugee. . . It brought home to me just how much we take for granted, like clean homes and clean water. . . It had never occurred to me how refugees would see England and its people and it definitely set me thinking. . .

Emma Roscoe

The Tiger in the Well by Philip Pullman (Viking) Runner-up, 1992
. . . My favourite part was when a mob of gansters had to look for Harriet, the baby . . . it was funny how none of the men knew what to do and gave it to the only woman present. . . My favourite character was Harriet. I liked the way that the author sometimes saw the story from her point of view. . . I would recommend this brilliant book to anyone over the age of thirteen because of the involvement with the Jews . . . quite hard to understand if you don't know anything about the Jewish Question. . .

Richard Robinson

The Granite Beast by Ann Coburn (Bodley Head) Short-listed, 1992
Ruth isn't your average fourteen-year-old because she never goes out, she never listens to music and doesn't have fashionable clothes. . . However, once you start reading it, it's a real matchsticks on the eyelids job!. . .

Josef Woodruff

The Book of the Banshee by Anne Fine (Hamish Hamilton) Short-listed, 1992
. . . tells the story of a 'war struck' family, seen through the eyes of a young teenage boy, Will Flowers. . . Estelle is a punk, who has everyone wrapped around her little finger. . . Her dad, who tries to keep on the good side of her . . . her mum, who sneaks in and out through the back window. . . Life goes on at 27 Beechcroft Avenue,

and life gets worse. . . Will would rather keep quiet than fight. But he may be the one to turn war into peace. . .
Christy Aylott

There are lessons to be learned from the reasons young critics gave for disliking a few of the nominated books, but I was interested to note that several novels were loved by some and hated by others. 'Long-winded', 'slow-moving' and 'boring' were among the more frequently aired complaints and there were many grumbles about books which started off well but soon began to drag. Some reviewers obviously felt cheated by disappointing endings to otherwise good stories, and others were put off by overly complicated plots, too many scientific details and 'difficult' words. Characters sometimes came under fire, too, for being wooden or unconvincing – 'not true to life'.

I can't resist including – for amusement only – a brief extract from the most damning criticism of all, made by schoolboy Michael Dobing'. . . DULL, UNEXCITING, BORING, NO ACTION, ADVENTURE, ROMANCE, COMEDY. . . Never get this unless you are blind, mad or sick. I think the book was written just to help people fall asleep.'

I wouldn't dream of revealing the title of the novel so graphically demolished by Michael, and feel it's only fair to add that it was praised as a 'HIT' by another reviewer. (Here we go again – you can't please 'em all.)

More about readers' opinions can be learned from the entertaining magazine, *In Brief*, edited by Elizabeth Hamill and obtainable from branches of Waterstone's bookshops. There are three issues a year of this journal, 'for teenagers by teenagers', and each contains candid reviews of new books, written by secondary school-children. Just as intriguing are the interview features – talks with favourite authors – and I strongly recommend the magazine to anyone seriously interested in writing for this market.

The young reader and adult novels

So far in this chapter I have stressed the importance of studying successful novels written specifically for young adults, but it would be impossible to paint an anywhere-near accurate picture of older children's reading preferences without paying proper attention to their tastes in adult fiction.

By discovering why so many ostensibly 'grown-up' books are popular with adolescents you'll gain a broader understanding of the concerns and demands of the fast-maturing young people you are aiming to please with a book of your own.

Recently, I brought this question up while lunching with eight 13-to-14-year-old pupils (four girls and four boys) from Forest School in Epping Forest. All I had been told about them beforehand was that they were avid readers, eager to put forward their views.

Although I'd been right in assuming most of them would enjoy detective fiction, I hadn't expected P.D. James to be discussed with such obvious enthusiasm. When one girl expressed her liking for Agatha Christie's books, I wondered if she also found them a little dated. 'But that's what makes them so interesting,' she said at once.

Historical novels were, in fact, popular with several pupils, along with fantasy and science fiction (Tolkien and Terry Pratchett). Others spoke of their enjoyment of the works of Antonia Fraser, Daphne du Maurier, Stephen King and Sue Townsend (*The Queen and I*). When we moved on to the subject of well-liked school set books, *The Thirty-Nine Steps* was mentioned, and so were *Animal Farm* and *Lord of the Flies*.

Of course they enjoyed magazines, too (*Just Seventeen* and some of the computer journals), but I left more determined than ever to urge my own readers to help stamp out the presumption that teenagers were interested only in pop stars, violence on television and high school romance.

Morals and taboos

Although accepting that it is impossible and not necessarily desirable to shield young people from the grislier facts of life, I'd like to express a few thoughts on the question of how much moral responsibility writers of young adult fiction should feel towards their readers. Please understand that I'm talking now only of authors intentionally aiming their work at the teenage market.

While it is becoming almost normal in adult novels for lovable charmers, dear old ladies included, to commit and get away with murder, it's a rather different matter when writers of teenage books glamorize or make heroes out of young crooks and thugs. Of course protagonists may dabble in crime, but I and many other writers agree that they should not escape scot-free and emotionally unscathed. Adolescents can be understandably bewildered by the 'bad is good' attitude of some modern television plays and films, and no caring author would wish, surely, to add to this confusion.

Always bear in mind that novels with 'teens' logos are well known to be popular with the under-twelves, who are naturally eager to come to grips with the adult world. Many of them enjoy identifying with the much older teenage characters in books and are fascinated by tales of sexual encounters, but it seems only fair for you, as a writer, to make sure your readers are aware of the risks involved.

Find ways of balancing realism with discretion. If and when you feel that your young lovers have reached the stage of a sexual relationship, proceed with caution and avoid going into explicit, step-by-step details. You are writing a story, remember, not a manual on the delights of sex.

It's also worth remembering that publishers – and book club selectors, too – with reputations to safeguard, are on the whole reluctant to consider novels for young adults which delve into matters as controversial as AIDS, promiscuity, under-age sex and homosexuality. Readers avidly interested in themes such as these will find them aplenty on the adult book and magazine shelves.

It might be helpful, when writing your novel, to ask yourself if you would be happy for your own and your friends' children to read it. Think, too, whether you would feel in any way embarrassed or guilty if they happened to discover that it had been written by you.

The awful 'isms'

Give some thought to these mostly derogatory terms as they creep one by one into everyday vocabulary: racism, classism, sexism and so on. It is no longer, thank heaven, the norm for heroes and heroines in children's literature to be middle-class and white-skinned. On the whole, nowadays, they address their parents as 'Mum' and 'Dad', and the terms 'Mummy' and 'Daddy' are used only by tiny tots and those self-styled aristocrats usually portrayed as figures of pity, curiosity or fun. Whatever your characters' background they should be aware of the people and goings-on in the world outside it. By all means let them discuss and think about different forms of snobbery and the pros and cons of single-sex and co-educational schools, but make sure that *you* have – and show – a modern outlook on such topics.

If you have any sexist attitudes yourself, keep them well out of your young-adult novels. I've only once been accused of sexism and that was a few months ago, when I took part in a talk with older pupils at a local primary school. The subject was popular reading matter and I turned up with a carrier-bag bulging with magazines to hand out at the end of the session. I felt a bit like Father Christmas as they all clamoured round me for their share of the goodies and everyone seemed quite happy at the time. A week later, though, I received a bundle of thank-you letters, including a reproachful note from one of the girl pupils, disapproving of the way I'd given the football papers to the boys in the class, and the magazines of seemingly feminine interest to the girls. The fact that I hadn't noticed myself doing this made me feel suitably ashamed – and determined to mend my ways.

2
The novel: planning, plotting and characterisation

Although it's unwise to take anything for granted in this writing game, I'd like to assume that by now you have the raw ingredients of a novel tumbling through your mind. Possibly you've been been wandering about in a daze for weeks, only vaguely aware of neighbourly greetings and oncoming traffic, developing your plot and bringing your characters to life inside your head. Maybe you've already started scribbling, and there's nothing bad about that, because everyone agrees that writing gets better with practice.

All the same, a certain amount of planning is advisable, and time-saving in the long-run, so try to resist the temptation to stampede too far into your first chapter before doing a little spadework to save yourself possible hassles later on. How *much* planning depends entirely on you and the type of person you are.

Working conditions

If you have a room in your home which you can set aside as your office, you are more fortunate than many, and if you own or can afford to buy something along the lines of a word processor (discussed in more detail on page 106) this will save you a great deal of time, frustration and fury – and so will a desk of your own.

Try not to be put off by lack of space and lavish equipment. Best-sellers have been produced by way of battered portable typewriters on kitchen and bedroom tables. Countless authors have made do, at one time or another, with cupboards or chests of drawers to keep papers and folders out of harm's way.

An ability to type *is* almost a necessity these days, as publishers are reluctant to consider handwritten manuscripts, however neatly presented. Possibly, though, you have someone willing to type out your work, and do bear in mind that many typists are self-taught. If you know you'd be happier writing your first draft by hand, rest assured that other novelists, Jean Ure and Pete Johnson among them, feel exactly the same way.

For some people, the big problem is finding peace and quiet to write. Try to get across to friends and family that your intention to write for teenagers is not some freaky new hobby and plan your working hours *with* them rather than against them. Once you've made a determined start, they may even show interest, help with research and protect you from intrusions.

Notes and notebooks

In a few (very few) how-to-write books you will find copious exercises intended to give you practice in character-building, writing dialogue and so on, along with advice about spending days on end writing preliminary notes covering every aspect of your book. If you are a highly methodical person, it might seem sensible and helpful to have a drawer full of carefully labelled notebooks. If you are not, remember that when studying any kind of work-to-rule manual, you are possibly reading the wholly personal views of just one writer. I know many successful authors prefer a considerably less organized approach, feeling that too much orderly planning is hampering, puts a curb on imaginative powers and spoils the adventure of creating work which is theirs and theirs alone.

To writers who have never tackled a novel before, I suggest that, as at start, at any rate, at least two notebooks are necessary. A loose-leaf, ring-clip A4 folder is useful for easy reference, and extra sheets of paper (from cheap, ready-punched pads, available from most stationers) can be slotted into the appropriate sections with the minimum of effort. Because I'm a disgraceful loser of documents, I try not to let my folder out of my flat – and the fact that it is fairly bulky helps me to resist any temptation to do so.

For taking out and about, a pocket or handbag-size notepad with a spiral spine is ideal. Use this when researching for facts in libraries, and also for jotting down ideas and flashes of inspiration – little gems of dialogue – whenever they occur to you. Unless you have a superhuman memory, you are in danger of losing sight of these if you don't make a note of them straight away. Some writers keep notepads by their bedside lamps, and this is not as crazy as it sounds, because brilliant ideas seem to have a habit of cropping up in the small hours. Leave them until morning and you have forgotten them for good. It takes very little time to transfer pages from the notepad to relevant sections of the loose-leaf folder, where they can be stapled in place and kept safely until needed.

If you are one of the highly methodical people mentioned earlier, this may seem a rather haphazard way of saving information for later use, but then you are possibly an expert at devising filing systems of your own and need no suggestions in this area from me or anybody else.

The title and names of characters

Giving your novel a name may seem as good a way as any of making creative headway, but it's by no means an essential first move, and any working title will do at this early stage. Meanwhile, carry on trying to find the right one – while mowing the lawn, waiting in queues or doing anything else which leaves your mind free but takes you away from your desk.

Obviously, a clever, imaginative title will tempt readers to pick at random from the shelves a book by a writer so far unknown to them. This is just one reason why titles deserve plenty of careful thought. An author may choose to give a hint of what to expect from the book itself: for example, while *Groosham Grange* (an award-winning novel by Anthony Horowitz) suggests a blend of spookiness and hilarity, *The Haunted Sand* (Hugh Scott) points to a more chilling type of ghost story. It's easy to imagine science fiction addicts making an eager grab for *Killer Planet* (Bob Shaw) and pop fans taking a second glance at *The Girl Who Got To No. 1* (Annalena McAfee). Some titles such as *I am the Cheese* and *The Chocolate War* (both by Robert Cormier) are quite intriguing enough to arouse interest and curiosity without giving anything away.

Check at a library or with a friendly, computerized book

seller whether your own chosen title has already been used, but even if it has not, you may eventually be asked to change it for one reason or another – perhaps because of its similarity to another title on the publisher's list.

Most writers prefer to give more urgent attention to the choosing of names for the characters in their book. I find this great fun – it helps enormously to bring them to life and is one of those games-for-one to play on a long journey. But again, care is needed.

Try to avoid names which have gained soapy popularity over the last twenty years or so: *Tracey* and *Sharon* are obvious examples. By all means bring old names back into vogue, but make sure they don't give your character a quaint, old-fashioned image (unless you *want* him or her to appear quaint and old-fashioned). Understandably, some young readers complain about names which are difficult to pronounce, though most of us would think twice, anyway, before lumbering a young heroine with, say, the Biblical tag of *Aholibamah*.

Longer, even cumbersome, names can be useful inasmuch as they are often shortened in different ways by different people, giving the reader a clearer picture of certain situations. A girl called Elisabeth by her teacher, may be Lisa to her parents and Liz to her mates; it is unlikely, nowadays, that she would be known as Beth or Betty, diminutives which would be better suited to great aunts and elderly neighbours.

Nicknames – the more original the better – may give useful clues to a character's personality, at the same time adding a spark of fun to your story. As a jokey example, a girl with the rather unfortunate name of Tessa Coe might well be known to her schoolmates as 'Tesco'.

You may have noticed in current teenage fiction, the tendency towards very short names. (I've seen Zak once or twice lately – no doubt short for Zachariah.) Some writers devise unusual spellings to attract immediate interest, and a bizarre character is often given an aptly zany name. Ploys such as these can be highly effective provided they are not overdone.

Quite probably you'll find yourself almost automatically picking names which seem to suit the personalities you have in mind, but if you're stuck for ideas, start reading the Births columns in daily newspapers, or skim through one of the recently published name-your-baby manuals available in libraries and bookshops.

The time of action: past, present or future

By now you will, no doubt, have decided when your story takes place. If you are writing a historical novel, you will either be knowlegeable about your chosen period or prepared to put in the study needed to avoid glaring inaccuracies. For a fantasy, set in the far-distant past or future, only you can predict how much knowledge, scientific or otherwise, you'll need – and *because* it's fantasy you are free, to some extent, to let your vivid imagination fill in the gaps.

You may well be feeling that a present day setting, for a first novel at any rate, is by far the safest option, but even this has its problems. When discussing her recent book, *A Place to Scream*, which is set in the very near future – 2015 – Jean Ure said, 'Nowadays, I can't keep up with the present. Everything keeps changing and a book can be dated even before publication date.'

Her sighs on this subject were very understandable. Although young people are often fascinated by tales of the past, most of them dread the thought of appearing old-fashioned themselves – hence their love of zany, up-to-the-minute clothes, expressions, crazes – and this is something to bear in mind. If you have neither the wish nor courage to adopt Jean's way of solving the dilemma – by moving the action twenty-odd years ahead of current events – console yourself with the fact that outstandingly good novels live on whether dated or not.

If you have fears that your book will survive only if it retains its up-to-the-minute appeal, consider the following suggestions – tricks of the trade – and you'll probably find yourself devising a few more of your own.

- Avoid, where possible, talking about true, modern-day events, such as royal scandals, as if these had only just happened. Let the characters remember back to them.

- Treat pop music in a similar way; if a Sixties hit plays a necessary part in your story, let it be discovered, perhaps, by way of a radio programme or an older person's cassette collection.

- Be wary of minor problems and controversies – smoking in certain public places, for instance – which may have changed by the time your book appears on the shelves.

- Remember – as if you could forget – that goverments can change overnight, almost. Ask yourself whether there is any real need to mention a politician by name. Be deliberately vague about facts which are not important to your plot.

- Invent your own fashion crazes instead of relying on the wilder trends currently sweeping the country. Fake fur headbands and smartie-dot leggings may be all the rage while you're planning your novel, but dead as clip-on earrings before you've finished writing it.

Plot outline

Even for those of us who shy away from the thought of writing reams of preparatory notes, there are some disciplines which shouldn't be shirked – because, as my old granny might have said, they are for our own good.

One of these is the typing or writing out of your plot outline: a summary of the story which has been playing and unfolding in your mind and is now ready for more orderly development. At this early stage, the outline is for you and you alone, so make it as long or short as you please, in note form if you like, but leave plenty of space between lines for scribbled alterations, improvements and second thoughts. Later on, you may want to write a formal synopsis for your chosen publisher (discussed on page 46) and this first, rough outline will be of great help when the time comes.

It will also enable you to assess the strength of your plot from an outsider's point of view. When reading it through, bear in mind that this storyline will have to be expanded into a book of say, 30 to 40 thousand words, and so ask yourself if it contains enough substance – drama, excitement, fun, pathos, conflict – to hold the readers' interest from beginning to end.

If you have doubts about this, consider the idea of

weaving a sub-plot into the main story – not for purposes of padding but to add intrigue, or possibly to lighten an overly grim basic theme.

Anyone who has attended a course on novel-writing will be familiar with the word *conflict*. Briefly this is the collective term used for the obstacles, from minor hassles to major disasters, which disrupt the progress of the protagonist on his or her road to success. Without conflict, there would be no story worth reading, for who would be enthralled by the smooth-running tale of a young athlete who won every heat without mishap before achieving the triumph of an Olympic medal? In this case, the necessary conflict might take the form of a broken ankle, lack of money or another character's sneaky efforts to bring about the athlete's disgrace and disqualification.

The real interest comes from the way the protagonist copes with the conflict. I still remember the advice given me by a wily old Scots picture-paper editor on the subject of compiling plots: 'Avoid fortuitous happenings'. By this he meant that problems should not be overcome merely by way of unexpected strokes of luck – that if a character desperately needed money, he should devise some way of earning it – the more original, the better. A cheque, out of the blue, from a long-lost uncle, would add neither interest nor credibilty to the story.

No amount of action and conflict, however skilfully handled, will compensate for an unsatisfactory ending to a novel, and this is something worth considering while mulling over your outline. Adults may merely be irritated by a novel's limply inconclusive final chapter, but younger readers, with less experience of such inadequacies, feel cheated and thoroughly let down.

This doesn't mean they expect every story to end happily with all loose ends tied up with Boy Scout precision. That's kids' stuff to teenagers, who are already learning the folly of expecting fairy-tale endings to *anything*. It means more that they deserve a rounded, thought-provoking finish to a book they have taken the trouble to read.

Whether your ending is tragic, jubilant, wistful or hilarious – don't let it be disappointing. Pay some attention to this now, to reduce the risk of a frantic re-think when you near the end of your novel.

The characters

Almost certainly, your plot outline will help you to become more familiar with your characters and the parts they play in the story. Now is the time to study their personalities in depth, to know them as well – and preferably better – than you know your close friends and relatives. As Dianne Doubtfire rightly pointed out in her handbook, *The Craft of Novel-Writing*, 'Creating imaginary characters is the core of novel-writing – and the possibilities are endless.'

You'll come to know and understand them even more thoroughly if you make a detailed pen portrait of each one in turn. It may be worth deciding upon their ages first, remembering that young readers, hungering for adult status, prefer sharing the adventures of protagonists slightly older than themselves. (A 12 or 13-year-old may like to think: 'That's how life will be for *me* when I'm 16 or 17.')

Write down everything else you have discovered, so far, about the characters in your book: their nationalities and background, looks and ambitions, loves and hates, good traits and bad. Consider how they interrelate to other people in the story, and decide whether you like them a little, a lot or not at all. If they behave badly, try to work out the reason for this. For example, a boy labelled a bighead by his mates may have adoring parents who hang on to his every word – but it is also possible that family members at home are forever belittling him – putting him down, treating him as a child – which might well give him the unconscious need to express himself rather too forcibly elsewhere.

However fond you become of your protagonists, take care to avoid making them too good to be true. If you appreciate them for their weaknesses as well as their strengths, they'll stand more chance of emerging as real, believable people, rather than as stereotyped heroes and heroines, impossibly sinless – and *boring* because of it.

Friendships between the main characters are sometimes more interesting if those concerned have noticeably different personalities. (We all know couples who seem hopelessly ill-matched, yet stay together in spite of – or because of – their differences.) Your readers will quite probably be in the throes of relationship problems of their own, so let them sympathize, empathize or disagree with the way your protagonists handle theirs. You may deliberately set out to encourage readers' disapproval of some of your characters, thus adding more conflict to your basic theme.

While male novelists in this field often talk happily of their heroines, women writers seem more reluctant to give the leading role to a boy. Annie Dalton (described by one reviewer as 'a daring writer') admitted that she, too, had had worries of this nature, but decided to treat them as a challenge. Discussing Owen, the main character in her recent novel, *Naming the Dark*, she said, 'I suppose he was something of an experiment and I wasn't altogether keen on him at first. But gradually I began to like him – and I always *will* like him now, I'm quite sure of that.'

The lesson here is that you shouldn't write off your capabilities until you've put them to the test.

As a rule, in younger children's books, parents are worthy citizens, loved and respected by their offspring, and it is only the likes of wicked stepmothers who are allowed to have flaws. This may be very right and proper, but it is not a rule you need observe when writing for young adults. Parents frequently form part of the emotional conflict and may be shoplifters, layabouts, marriage-breakers, or just out of prison. Of course they don't *have* to be bad, or even misguided, and they needn't be middle-aged has-beens, either. It's worth remembering that the mother of a 15-year-old girl may still be in her thirties, with a keen interest in fashion and an enviably modern outlook. (Perhaps *too* modern for comfort providing further conflict.)

It has been said that the strength of a novel lies in its villain and, whether or not this is true, there is no denying that good story-tellers are often particularly good at creating memorable villains. These baddies may evoke feelings of hatred, terror, scorn and, perhaps, pity; sometimes they are so awful they are funny, which is fine provided the writer intends them to be funny. It is, of course possible for sinners to mend their ways, but the change from bad to good has to be convincing, and a character who was positively evil in Chapter One is unlikely to become a whiter-than-white saint by the end of the book. Villains have a place in fiction just as they have in everyday life, and in both cases it may be advisable to treat them with caution.

I am often surprised at the way non-writing friends like to assume that my characters are based on people I know. The main reason why they are not – apart from the obvious risks of being sued for libel – is that I would feel uncomfortably restricted if I were not totally in control of my own characters. As part of my story, they have to think and act as *I* think fit, and several of my writer friends are familiar with this feeling. Some of them compare their characters to the 'imaginary friends' they dreamed up in early childhood – who were as alive, in their way, as the kids next door.

The truth is that however well we know the people around us, we have no way of reading their minds, and what they say is not necessarily what they mean. Of course they stimulate ideas, and there are bound to be similarities, but on the whole it is far less complicated and infinitely more satisfying to create personalities of our own.

Viewpoint and tense

You may be wondering whether to write your novel solely from your main character's point of view. For purposes of simplification only, let's make her a girl in this instance, and call her Sophie.

Because teenagers enjoy identifying with the protagonists in a book, stories written in the first person ('I opened the door worriedly. . . I sensed trouble the moment I saw him . . . .') are often highly popular. If you decide to hand your story over, as it were, to Sophie, you'll give your readers an immediate feeling of intimacy – provided, that is, that *you* feel happy writing first person narrative. The simple way to find out is by scribbling out an experimental page or two to discover how comfortable you feel with this particular style.

You may feel it is too restricting – that Sophie will only be able to talk of her own thoughts and describe events which she herself has witnessed – but there are ways round limitations such as these. Clever use of dialogue is one of them: other characters may express their feelings to Sophie, tell her of their experiences and repeat remarks made to them behind her back. She may overhear telephone conversations, read a letter addressed to someone else, sense how people are feeling without being told. She doesn't *have* to be gazing purposefully in a mirror in order to describe her appearance; she may catch sight of her dishevelled brown hair in a shop window, comment glumly on a photograph of herself, refuse to borrow a friend's skirt because it doesn't suit her tall, skinny figure, pale complexion – or whatever. Set your imagination to work, study other's writers' handling of first person narrative, and most of the problems will fade away.

If you enjoy writing in the first person, but would prefer to have the viewpoints of more than one leading character, consider the possibility of sharing the limelight between them. Pete Johnson used this technique very successfully in his novel, *We The Haunted*, by allocating his protagonists separate, sometimes alternating, chapters, thus enabling them to air differing opinions in their own, easily recognizable ways.

With third person narrative ('Sophie opened the door . . . she sensed trouble . . .'), roughly the same rules apply *provided* the book is written from just one person's viewpoint. If you have several main characters, think carefully before allowing two or more of them to think or muse to themselves in any one chapter. For instance, if you are anxious for the villain to put across his feelings about certain people or events, give him his own chapters or sections in which to do so. If you don't, the reader may become hopelessly confused and lose thread of the story altogether.

You may dislike the idea of 'viewpoint characters' and prefer the narrator (you) to tell the story as it happens, remaining totally detached from the characters themselves. This technique is often used in adult novels, but is not so popular with younger readers, who seem to prefer the involvement of a less aloof approach.

In the same way, many teenagers feel uneasy about books written in the present tense, quite possibly because they are so much more familiar with past-tense stories. Back to Pete Johnson – who discovered this preference when discussing with a few of his young critics the first draft of a suspense story. 'Not all of them,' he admitted, 'experienced the sense of immediacy I'd felt and enjoyed, myself, when using the present tense.'

Style and humour

Your style is your own, a crucial part of your talent for writing. I've yet to be convinced that style can be learned by way of a book or any other form of tuition, but I'll stress again my belief that the quality of almost every writer's work improves with practice. If you enjoy experimenting, so much the better. I have already discussed the value of reading and comparing books by successful authors, and it also helps, to have a good basic knowledge of grammar and punctuation, even if you don't obey all the rules all the time. (More about this in Chapter Seven).

The quality of humour is even harder to define, but I think it's fair to say that comedians are born, not made; I don't believe anyone can be taught to be funny.

The easy ability to make readers laugh is perhaps the most envied of all writing skills. Don't try too hard, because forced humour is usually too irritating to be funny, and it's a mistake to use exclamation marks merely as a way of indicating that you are in a lighthearted mood. Don't worry if you're not a natural comic; unless you take a relaxed attitude, your own brand of humour won't stand a chance.

Length

The usual length of teenage novels is something between 30,000 and 40,000 words, but look on that as a very rough guide. Books in the popular series I've mentioned are often even shorter, and if you're thinking of writing one of these, try to discover the required length from the publisher concerned. Either write a brief letter of enquiry (enclosing, as always, a stamped, addressed envelope), or make a similarly brief phone call. You might ask, at the same time, whether there are openings in that particular series for British authors. I don't often advise telephone calls, but if you make it plain that you're merely seeking information, it will also be clear that you're saving the time and trouble of letters to and fro.

Strictly accurate word counts are rarely, if ever asked for. Some word processors provide them at the press of a button or two, but if you know the average number of words which you and your machine produce, per page, you'll be able to keep an eye on the length of your work.

Chapter-by-chapter analysis

The breakdown of a plot into chapters is, as often as not, the final stage of preliminary planning, and it will help you to decide whether or not you have the makings of a balanced novel. Look upon it as a useful but flexible guide, because you will undoubtedly want to make alterations and improvements while writing and re-writing during the weeks ahead.

By setting aside a separate page in your loose-leaf notebook for each chapter, you'll save bothersome time when making amendments or changing the order of action.

The true beginning of your story need not coincide with the happenings in Chapter One. The first chapter should be designed to grasp and hold on to the interest of readers, and may legitimately contain far more than its share of intrigue and suspense. Try to begin at a point of high drama – an important change, perhaps, in your main character's life – and work out how the events leading up to this may be covered in subsequent chapters.

Take each chapter in turn, jotting down necessary snippets of action and progressing the story in note form. When you've finished, read through this second, more detailed plot outline very carefully and consider these questions:

- Are the episodes of excitement/fear/amusement evenly distributed throughout the book?
- Are there parts with too much description and too little action?
- Will it be possible to end the first and at least some other chapters on a note of suspense, creating curiosity and an incentive to read on?
- Is there an even balance between very short and longer chapters?
- Is there room in each chapter for character development and the snatches of dialogue which will help more than anything to bring your characters and story to life?

Consider and re-consider until you are aching to begin – to write the heading, 'Chapter One' on a blank sheet of paper. Most importantly of all, bear in mind these words of advice from Lindsey Fraser of the Book Trust 'Whatever your theme, give first priority to the telling of a rattling good story.'

3

The novel: writing, revising and the business of selling

If this is your first novel, try to resign yourself to the probability that few publishers will consider it seriously until they have seen the finished book.

I discussed this with several commissioning editors and although they agreed that they would be unlikely to talk of contracts before reading the completed novel, Victoria Eldon put forward the option of submitting three chapters and a carefully worked-out synopsis of the plot (See page 46) to a chosen publisher in the hope of an enouraging response.

If you decide to take up this suggestion, enclose a *very* brief covering letter and a stamped addressed envelope large enough for the return of your manuscript. Weeks may pass before you receive a reply, but it is just possible that the publisher will like your story-so-far, and invite you to submit the completed work in due course. It is highly improbable that there will be any mention of a contract at this stage, but if you are given a few words of advice – on length, perhaps, or treatment of your theme – you'll have have good reason to feel heartened. Most importantly, don't give up hope if your work is rejected, but take note of any reasons given and keep correspondence of this kind in a folder for future reference.

People who write their first drafts by hand often like to type each chapter out (or put it on to a disk) and edit as they go, but there are no set rules and you'll soon find a routine to suit yourself. These days I work straight on to my word processor and I've learned the hard way to obey the golden rule of transferring each day's work to a back-up disk. There are few things more heartbreaking than the loss, through the vagaries of a machine, of a chapter, or even a page of a book. (Before I became computerized, I made use of carbon papers or photocopiers, for the sake of my peace of mind.)

You'll find more information on submitting your work – synopses, presentation, contracts, agents and so on – in the second part of this chapter, but meanwhile let's return to the more urgent business of writing, construction and hard, hard work.

Page one, Chapter one

As an aid to selling, the first page of your novel is surely the most important of all. It is quite usual for readers of any age to rely on a quick appraisal of the opening lines by way of deciding whether or not they will enjoy – and therefore buy or borrow – a book.

I have already advised you to aim, early on in a novel, at attracting and holding readers' attention and now I'm urging you to put all you've got into arousing *instant* interest in paragraph number one. And two and three. . .

Once more, it is impossible for me to give specific advice because I know nothing of your plot, so I'll try to conjure up inspiration by commenting on examples of established writers' work. If you consider and compare these when investigating the whys and wherefores of good beginnings, they may set you thinking of ways to inject readability-plus into your own opening sentences. All young people, even the exceptionally laid back, seem fascinated by talk of air travel, associating it with faraway places, jet-setters and adventures into the unknown. The start of a journey often makes a compelling start to a story and this first paragraph of Will Gatti's *Absolute Trust* skilfully sets the scene for a transatlantic thriller, taut with suspense from the very first word.

> 'Ding.' The FASTEN SEAT BELT hologram appeared over the middle aisle and the plane tilted slightly. Outside was nothing but solid grey. Moments later the grey began to shred, and with some excitement Talent peered across his neighbours to see snatches of ground below.

The use of Talent's surname makes it plain that there is to be no childish nonsense about this book, and yet before the end of the first page, we learn that Talent is a 17-year-old boy on his first flight 'across an ocean'. So here, young readers may feel, is a story for adults which they, too, will enjoy.

For teenagers who are seeking signs of humour, the

opening paragraph of Paul Zindel's *The Pigman* offers a tempting foretaste of an unorthodox treat in store.

> Now, I don't like school, which you might say is one of the factors that got us involved with this old guy we nicknamed the Pigman. Actually, I hate school, but then again most of the time I hate everything.

The message here is clear, encouraging self-styled misfits to read on – and as many young adults prefer to think of themselves as misfits, it's no wonder Zindel's books are popular.

Mary Hooper introduces her own brand of wit and sense of fun at the beginning of her book, *Making Waves*, and her use of lighthearted dialogue adds to the promise of an entertaining read.

> 'Now, are you quite sure about this hairdressing college business?' Mum asked, pausing from unpacking the week's shopping on to the kitchen table.
>
> 'Of course I am!' I said. 'Anyway, it's all arranged.'
>
> 'I mean, a nice secretarial course would set you up for life. Shorthand and typing are always useful.'
>
> 'In a hairdressing salon?' I said, looking at Mum pityingly. 'Oh yes, I suppose if someone came in for a haircut I could always persuade them to have a letter typed instead.'

Compare this extract with the introductory paragraphs of another career story: Lorna Read's *City Sax*.

> 'Too much air,' he informed her curtly. 'You're blowing too hard. Blow more softly. And your lips are far too tense. They should be like an elastic band, flexible, not too loose nor too tight. And there should never be any sounds coming from your mouth – that's what the instrument's for. Look, put it down for a minute. Flex your fingers. Shake your shoulders, you're standing like a soldier at attention!'
>
> Chris did as he said, feeling utterly depressed. There was nothing worse than thinking you were pretty good at something and then being told that you were doing it all wrong, she thought.

You'll notice how both these writers bring in almost simultaneously their leading characters and strong hints of what to expect from the stories which follow. The career themes are there, right from the start – but in Lorna's Read's opening dialogue we have a more intense and dedicated approach to her chosen subject, no doubt designed to attract young readers already keenly interested in the world of popular music.

In tales of fantasy, science fiction and the supernatural, some writers like to begin in a deceptively relaxed and everyday manner, relying on the cover illustration and blurb to satisfy readers' curiosity about the eerier contents of the book.

In *Naming the Dark*, Annie Dalton lets her likeable, apparently unexceptional schoolboy protagonist provide first-page interest, and ever-so gradually she builds up the suspense into a crescendo of macabre suspicion at the end of the chapter.

> Owen Fisher was killing time until the party trying to decide whether to wear his white shirt with the plain black waistcoat from Second-Hand Rose, or the fancy Edwardian one his grandfather Cy had grudgingly sold him for a tenner a couple of years ago.

Books in horror-story series tend to begin as they mean to go on, as shown here in the opening lines of the prologue of *The Witness*. Notice how author, Jesse Harris, uses the immediacy of the present tense – discussed in the previous chapter – and disquieteningly staccato sentences to add to the overall chill.

> *It's ten o'clock.* The house is quiet. A tall teenage girl climbs the stairs. A long black braid hangs down her back. She checks on the children. They are all asleep.

To give aspiring writers of horror series another hint of what might be expected of them, here are the final lines of this one-and-a-half-page prologue.

> He pushes her back. She falls to the floor. It's cold and damp. The knife flashes above her. The man's eyes are closed. The knife plunges down.

First signs of life

Don't worry unduly if it takes hours of frustrating work – rejecting and reconsidering – before you are completely satisfied with your opening. It's very rare for a writer to get the feel, and into the swing, of a book straight away. Take heart from Pete Johnson's thoughts on this matter, expressed on the cover of *We The Haunted*:

> Writing the first page – I dread that! Every book is a battle. I have pads full of notes but my characters only come alive when they hit the page. I have to let them run around for a few pages to get to know them better.
>
> Just as I'm wishing I'd never started, the characters suddenly take off. I can't stop thinking or talking about them (as my friends know). They even drop into my dreams. That's why there's a notepad by my alarm clock.

In the same way that your writing brings your characters to life, so will your characters bring life to your book. Although it's advisable to bring your protagonist(s) into being on that crucial first page, introduce other characters gradually, for fear of confusing readers with too many names and people.

Draw particular attention to characters who will sooner or later play an important part in the plot. Mention any unusual or significant characteristics and, perhaps, give them something to say.

Dialogue

It is no exaggeration to say that a novel – and a teenage novel in particular – can stand or fall by the quality of its dialogue. There are so many reasons for this, it would be impossible to discuss them all, but here are a few points worth considering on the values of well-written dialogue:

- It is a way of progressing the story, often obviating the need for lengthy description.

- Characters are more easily understood when given plenty of opportunities to talk and express their thoughts in conversation. People in real life are frequently judged by the way they speak and the things they say. (And I'm not thinking merely of regional and 'foreign' accents.)

- Good dialogue makes for readability. It is perhaps the easiest way to inject a spark of humour into a book, and is often used effectively as a way of lightening a depressingly heavy situation.

You may think that the first essential is for a character to talk realistically, but care is needed here. In everyday conversation, people tend to talk round subjects, hesitate, repeat themselves, falter and begin again. In fiction, such beating about the bush can come across as tedious and, in some cases, ridiculous.

Take this (deliberately exaggerated) example . . . Someone in real life, blustering his way round an argument, might say: 'I don't know what you're getting at. You keep going on and on – well, I mean, it doesn't make sense. I mean – for heaven's sake – what are you trying to say?'

There's no room in written dialogue for this kind of rambling, and much more of it would try the patience of a saint, let alone a 12-year-old schoolboy, impatient to know what's coming next. The same character would do better to cut the cackle and say: 'Get to the point, can't you?'

To some writers, dialogue comes easily and they seem able, almost, to hear what their characters are saying. Others are less fortunate and find it necessary to read passages out loud to themselves to make sure they ring true. As always, the more practice you put in, the more adept you'll become.

Once you begin to enjoy writing dialogue, you'll know you're making headway, and will probably start using it more and more, to vary the pace of your story and bring individuality to your characters, even those of the same age and sex.

Dialogue is a method of highlighting different situations. A 14-year-old girl is likely to have one way of talking to her mother, another when jabbering with her mate and a third when in conversation with a teacher. And how will she sound when trying to attract the interest of a boy she hardly knows?

Be careful not to put middle-aged expressions – such as 'Look here!' – into young adult mouths. Something along the lines of, 'Watch it!' has a truer, more convincing ring.

Don't be afraid of the word 'said'. Some writers of lightweight teenage fiction seem to to feel obliged to invent outlandishly expressive substitutes for this and other of the good old English verbs traditionally used in dialogue. The result is sometimes not quite, but almost, as appalling and mind-boggling as the example I've concocted here:

'You're lying!' hurled Jane.

'Don't deny it!' Paula shrilled.

'She's only pretending,' supplied Denise.

'I – I hate you all,' Sara choked.

Attempts such as this to be original merely distract readers' attention from the gist of the conversation. Of course it's acceptable for characters to *sneer* and *drawl* and *groan* occasionally; it's when the practice is overdone that it becomes intolerable. The sparing use of qualifying adverbs sometimes makes for less obtrusive dialogue. (E.g. 'Keep quiet,' James muttered tensely . . . instead of 'Keep quiet,' James gritted.)

Worse still, in my opinion, is the flagrant abuse, still fairly prevalent in cheaper paperback romances, of the verbs 'smile' and 'grin', e.g. 'I'm glad we met,' grinned John.

This is the kind of sloppiness which gives teenage fiction a 'bad fairy' reputation. The silly thing is, there are so many unobjectionable alternatives. Using a full stop instead of a comma, we'd have 'I'm glad we met.' John grinned.' Or just as simply 'I'm glad we met,' John said, grinning. Of course there's much to be learned from other writers' handling of dialogue, but it pays to be critical, too.

There is no rigid rule about single or double quotation marks. Provided you are consistent, use either (or the style favoured by the publisher to whom you intend to send your novel). For 'quotes within quotes', use double quotations marks within single, and vice versa, e.g. 'Gran kept crying "Help me!" ' Maggie told the doctor.

For reasons of clarity, particularly in novels for younger readers, each speaker should be given a new paragraph in which to have his say. (Again, this is not a rigid rule but it seems, on the whole, to be a sensible one.) In a conversation between just two people, dialogue tags ('said Philip' – 'replied Jane') are not always necessary, provided you make it obvious which one of them is talking. Use of a character's name may help here – e.g. 'Where are you going, Phil?'

Jargon and offensive language

'How do you cope with current jargon?' Writers in other fields often ask me this question, and I have to confess it poses problems which can't altogether be solved by keeping in constant contact with young people.

The reason, of course, is that teenage jargon is never 'current' for long. For instance, I hear that 'oldie-goldie' (meaning hopelessly dated) is all the rage at present, but by the time this book is published, it will no doubt have been replaced by a new verbal instrument of derision – and have become 'oldie-goldie' itself. To add to the confusion, my very enjoyable research into the matter revealed that buzz words of this kind varied not merely from area to area, but from school to school.

One safe solution is to avoid competing too fiercely. Be deliberately sparing in your use of trendier-than-trendy *in*-words; these are usually short-lived simply because they are over-used: picked up by yuppies and flogged out of existence by chat show presenters. The term 'brill' is now dead to all but jolly-hockey-sticks aunties and junior school comic-readers – but the less sensationalistic 'brilliant' and 'great' seem to linger on, year after year.

Jean Ure dodges the dilemma by devising jargon of her own. 'Sometimes I delve into the past and bring back expressions which were popular before any of us were born,' she told me.

Everyone slips up now and then, but mistakes of this kind are easily put right, and no publisher is likely to turn down an outstandingly good novel simply because it contains a mere handful of out-of-date words.

With good reason, you may be more anxious to learn ways of avoiding offensive language when trying to write convincing dialogue. The plain truth, as we all know, is that many teenagers, when arguing among themselves – and especially when spoiling for a fight – tend to use near-obscenities in every other sentence. So now we're back to the touchy matters of readers' demands, writers' responsibilities and publishers' reputations.

People have been known to protest that it is not the readers, but their parents, teachers and other adults in authority, who are disturbed by the use of swear words, etc. in teenage literature. In common with other lofty generalizations, this is a boring argument, and most children's writers prefer to steer clear of adult disapproval – mainly, I suspect, because they are civilized adults themselves. 'I hate to hear a child swear,' my mother used to say when I was small, and it's easier to respect her feelings now than it was at the time.

I discussed with novelist Mary Hooper the difficulties of translating unprintable badinage into acceptable repartee – how expressions such as 'For heaven's sake!' so often seemed pathetically watered-down versions of what might actually have been said. She suggested one way round this was to create dialogue strong enough to stand on its own without need of unpalatably lurid reinforcement. (After all there's nothing to stop you inventing inoffensively lurid expressions as passable substitutes for the real thing.)

This is not to say that you should mislead readers into believing that the language used by your characters is always above reproach. That's the kind of hypocrisy which teenagers despise, and with good reason. Instead, let the narrative play its part, doing the dirty work for you – for example 'Martin swore viciously as he shoved his way forward' – or 'As their curses grew more and more obscene . . .' Use your imagination in one way and another and leave your readers to rely on theirs to fill in the gaps.

It also pays to be sparing with the use of heavy dialect (regional accents and so on). Too much is distracting and tedious to decipher. A smattering, here and there, is fine, but tread warily. In the same way, if yours is a historical novel, guard against archaic, unnatural-sounding 'prithee fair maid' nonsense, but at the same time watch out for laughably inappropriate space-age expressions such as 'Wow – it's supersonic!'

Moving the story ahead

Some of the plot-building examples given in this section may seem rather on the banal side, but please realize that I am trying to cater for a wide variety of needs. Look on them not so much as suggestions but more as ways to help you stimulate ideas and ruses of your own.

If, in order to grab immediate interest, you've set your first chapter at some point of high drama in the story, be careful not to give too much away, too soon. Concentrate on building up the suspense – make the most of imminent danger, eerie surroundings, menacing characters – but give no unnecessary clues about how the mystery may or will be solved. If, for instance, your protagonists, Jake and Tess, are at the mercy of crooks, it might be wiser not to mention that, in the background, two of their friends are busily plotting ways of rescuing them. If they are on a sinking boat, don't let on that either Jake or Tess has recently won a lifesaver's medallion. If you suggest ways out of a predicament, the story is in danger of falling flat later on, simply because the reader knows what to expect and has no surprises in store.

Try to conclude each chapter on a note of intrigue. Many readers break off for tea or sleep at the end of a chapter, so give them plenty of incentive to return to the book; make them curious to discover what happens next.

If, in the second chapter, you begin covering the events which led up to your dramatic opening, find a way to be sure your readers are aware of this, for example 'It all began when. . .' Consider also the flashback technique described on pages 60–1

Indirect dialogue is sometimes a useful method of speeding up the action. The sentence, 'She told Dave how to program the video', might do away with the need for wearisome verbal instructions on the workings of a particular recorder; unless important to the plot in some other way, details of this kind are of no concern whatsoever to the majority of readers.

Consider ways in which your characters' individual personalities will add interest to the developing story. A boy with no sense of time may arrive too late to take part in an important event . . . a girl who is terrified of heights may fake a sprained ankle to avoid taking part in a mountaineering expedition . . . and so on.

Sometimes it is useful to emphasize a stressful situation by way of a protagonist's out-of-character behaviour. A normally diligent or studious girl may become slapdash and apparently uncaring when her parents are threatening to separate. Family problems may – if only temporarily – turn a meek, law-abiding boy into an aggressive rule-breaker. Basically honest characters have been known to lie through their teeth in loyal defence of people close to them.

How much time you spend on your novel depends on your own circumstances, but it's worth trying to write a little – if only a few sentences – each day. By doing this you are less likely to lose track of the plot and the feel of your story; the longer you stay away from it, the harder it is to get back into the swing.

A few writers prefer to leave all thoughts of revision until they have completed a first draft, others revise as they go – and most of us do a little of each. Certainly it is advisable to keep a watchful eye on the progress of your work, reading it over from time to time for early detection of minor flaws in the plot.

I often find myself skimming through previous chapters over my early morning pints of tea. This encourages me to get straight down to work, and I know I'm more likely to spot mistakes and plot-inconsistencies after a reasonably good night's sleep than when I'm flaking with exhaustion at the end of a 14-hour working day.

After finishing each chapter and editing it as best I can for the time being, I like to print it out. This is partly because my work seems more real, somehow, when it's safely on paper, but also because I tend to miss quite glaring errors on screen. Maybe I'm old-fashioned, still not entirely at ease with computers, but there it is.

As you proceed with your novel, it's almost inevitable that you'll want to make changes to your original theme, and it may be useful to jot down the gist of these on the relevant section of your chapter-by-chapter analysis. This will help you to assess whether they improve your story or merely add complications which may be difficult to cope with later.

Later? Weeks may stretch into months of toil before you realize – sometimes rather suddenly, almost as if by chance – that the end is in sight. Mysteries are solved, villains are dealt with. Characters may have changed in some way as a result of their experiences in your story; in fact it is usually important that they *have* changed, in outlook if nothing else.

In the previous chapter I discussed endings – happy, sad, thought-provoking – in some detail, but now there is one more point I'd like to make. While writing about them, you may have become very fond of some of your characters, so fond that you are unwilling to say goodbye for ever. You may even be wondering about the possibility of bringing them together again in another story, another book; a sequel, in fact. This is probably something you'd prefer not to think too hard about at this stage for all sorts of reasons, but at least you can leave one or two of your options open.

If your main characters live in the same area, you'll have few problems provided you haven't killed them off or removed two of them to Australia, but if not, you might have them expressing thoughts and wishes about meeting again, sometime, somewhere, somehow. Once again, because I know nothing of your plot, I can't be more specific, but you'll no doubt enjoy devising possibilities of your own.

The end

These are magic words and my sensations of relief and exultation whenever I write them are quite indescribable.

Suddenly it doesn't matter that I'm completely exhausted; by some miracle the story has been written from beginning to end.

Of course there is more editing and revising to be done, visits to libraries to check over facts, but this is pleasing work for most writers because they are reading and improving upon their own creations. Re-typing is tedious, I agree, but a million times less irksome than typing out someone else's business letters.

Preparing your work for a publisher

After all the effort you've put into your novel, you would be crazy to ignore the basic rules of presentation when submitting the work to your chosen publisher. These are followed by nearly all established writers and there are good reasons for most of them.

- Use A4 paper of fairly good quality – neither flimsy nor ostentatiously thick – typing on one side only of each sheet.
- Always use double spacing, which makes for easier reading and provides space for an editor's corrections and instructions to the printer. Don't leave extra space between paragraphs unless you wish to indicate a natural break in the narrative.
- Leave margins at the sides and top and bottom of each page (at least 1–1½ inches on the left-hand side to allow for the use of printing equipment.)
- Use black typewriter ribbons and take care to change them the moment they show signs of wear.
- Begin each chapter on a new page, with its name or number centred at the top – e.g. 'Chapter Five'.
- Beneath the last sentence of your final chapter, type the words, 'ends' and add your name and address at the foot of the page.
- Read through the work from start to finish, making sure that minor corrections are neatly printed in ink. Some retyping may be necessary, where alterations appear messy or unclear and spoil the look of your manuscript.
- Check that the pages are correctly numbered (top right hand side is usual) from the beginning to the end of the book – i.e. don't start each chapter with a new set of numbers.
- Prepare a title page – the unnumbered, first page of your manuscript. At the top, type something along the lines of

'Teenage Novel, approx. 30,000 words'. The title of your book should appear in the centre of the page with your name or pseudonym beneath it, e.g. 'by Mary Nicholls'. At the foot of the page type your (real) name and address.

Synopses

Even when submitting a completed novel, some writers like to include a synopsis, hoping that if a commissioning editor is attracted by the storyline, he or she will show more interest and read on. This is entirely up to you; if yours is an unusual, very original theme, you may feel it's worth the effort. Make the synopsis as short as possible – a couple of hundred words, say – and use the present tense. In the first paragraph, give a summary of the basic plot and then continue with a tightly written, compact outline of the story.

If you intend to begin by submitting two or three chapters and a synopsis, your outline will have to be more detailed, but the keep-it-brief advice still applies. Use your original chapter-by-chapter analysis to help you with this, and aim to give the editor every reason to believe that the novel has been carefully planned from start to finish. As a general rule, leave no unconvincing, loose ends, but avoid wearisome descriptions, explanations and lengthy extracts from the book.

Submitting your work

As a start, instead of sending your complete mansucript, you may prefer to send a letter to your chosen publisher, writing a paragraph or two about your novel (basic theme, length etc.) asking if you may submit it, and enclosing a stamped addressed envelope for his or her reply. (Check the publisher's address and the relevant department in *Writers' and Artists' Yearbook or The Writer's Handbook*.)

You may not receive an immediate reply (that's the way it is, in publishing) but when you do hear, at least you will know – before going to the expense of posting a heavy package – whether or not that particular publisher is currently considering books of the kind you've written.

If you'd prefer to send the complete manuscript to the publisher, enclose a covering letter and a self-addressed label, adequately stamped for its return. Again, the letter should be very short: just give the title of your novel and ask for it to be considered. For your own peace of mind, you may like to include a stamped addressed (otherwise blank) postcard, requesting acknowledgment of your manuscript's safe arrival.

Don't use paper clips or staples to fasten sections of your work. Place the lot in a lightweight cardboard box, or a student's plastic folder, perhaps. Padded 'Jiffy' bags save time when parcelling – and you may feel it's worth making use of 'registered' or 'recorded delivery' postal services.

All this sounds a terrible palaver – and expensive, too – but it's how things are done in these difficult days. And to repeat an earlier warning – please, please be sure you have your own 'good' copy of your manuscript before sending it *anywhere*. To lose your only one would be tragic – to be faced with the task of re-typing from a messy draft or carbon copies would be horrendous.

The publisher's decision

From now until for ever. . . Quite likely, this is how you'll feel while waiting to know whether the publisher is interested in your book. It may be several months before you hear the verdict, and if you resign yourself to this – begin another novel, involve yourself in some other task – you won't be waiting on tenterhooks each morning for the postman to arrive.

If, after three or four months, you've heard nothing, by all means write a polite little letter to the publisher, just to make sure your work is being considered, but try very hard to resist the urge to make telephone queries. These very often do more harm than good.

Of course you'll feel devastated if your book is rejected; practically every living writer knows or remembers the feeling well. It has happened to nearly all of us at one time or another, best-selling authors included. Times are tough, remember. Naturally you're disappointed, but don't feel you're a failure. Be bloody, bold and resolute, as Macbeth was advised, admittedly in somewhat different circumstances – and *try another publisher*.

You'll have still less reason for despair if the rejection letter contains a few suggestions or words of encouragement. It is neither obligatory nor even usual for a publisher to comment on an unsolicited manuscript, so take note of any advice given and feel spurred on by this glimmer of hope when you get back to work.

As for the moment of mingled triumph and incredulity when a publisher shows interest in your work and makes vague mention of a contract . . . All I'll say is that it's well worth waiting for.

This book is about writing, and I don't want to stray too far into the business side of authorship: contracts, copyright and so on. Nevertheless, I want to stress how important it is for writers who have reached the stage of sales negotiations to be aware, to some extent at least, of the workings of the publishing proefession. When offered a contract, for instance, you should know what you're signing.

Described by the Society of Authors as 'invaluable reading', Michael Legat's handbook, *An Author's Guide to Publishing* provides a wealth of essential information for writers. It is also immensely readable. Of particular interest is the chapter describing what happens to your manuscript once you have submitted it to a publisher – explaining in detail, for example, *why* everything takes so long. There are sections on legal matters, royalties, multiple submissions, super accurate word-counts, desk-top and vanity publishing, selling abroad – and, of course, contracts and copyright.

Literary agents

Of course it helps to have a good agent, with contacts throughout the publishing world and expert knowledge of the market and marketing, whose job it is to handle the business side of your work. She (or he) is responsible for the submitting of manuscripts, the negotiating of contracts, royalties and advances, foreign and paperback rights – and much, much more.

Unfortunately you may have difficulty in persuading an agent to take you on unless you have something fairly impressive to show her in the way of previously published work. I know how unfair this sounds – rather a chicken-and-egg situation – but it would be unfair of *me* to mislead you into thinking that the services of literary agents are there for the asking. For survival, remember, they rely on the commission earned on their sales, so they have understandably good reason to be selective.

'I am here, first and foremost to sell saleable material,' literary agent, Maggie Noach, told me, after saying she was at present finding herself forced to turn down over 90 per cent of applications from would-be clients. 'So many writers of teenage fiction simply haven't made any preliminary study of this changing market for themselves.'

It is by no means impossible for an unknown writer to overcome the hurdle by approaching an agent with an outstandingly well written piece of work. If you'd like to try, but don't how to start, study the 'Literary Agents' sections in *The Writer's Handbook* or *Writers' and Artists' Yearbook*. (Many reputable agents are members of The Association of Authors' Agents, and their entries in these books are starred.) The accepted practice is to send a preliminary letter with an example (synopsis and first chapter, perhaps) of the book you are currently writing, along with a few carefully selected photocopies of previously published work, if any.

It's quite possible to succeed without an agent – so don't listen to pessimistic friends who tell you that proper attention is rarely if ever given to manuscripts in slush piles (the popular name for trays heaped with unsolicited manuscripts). This is simply not true; publishers know only too well that if they ignore those slush piles, they risk losing the chance, however remote, of adding a future best-selling author to their lists.

4

Short story collections and magazine fiction

SHORT STORIES

If, as a new writer, you have an unswerving aim to write fiction, but feel daunted by thoughts of a full-length novel, you may be mulling over the idea of a collection of short stories. Certainly you'd benefit from experimenting with style and technique: viewpoint, tense, and humour, for example. At the risk of sounding horribly depressing, however, I must warn you that it is far from easy – some say almost impossible – for an unknown writer to persuade a commissioning editor to accept a collection of his or her stories for publication in book form. Such anthologies do exist, but they are nearly all written by known authors whose names play a large part in promoting sales.

I spoke to several publishers about this and two of them offered a tiny spark of hope when saying that if, while planning a collection of stories based on a given theme – tales of detection, horror, romance or the supernatural, say – they happened to receive an outstandingly good and relevant story by an unknown writer, they might consider including it. This sounds a very chancey method of approach, but on occasions it has worked.

Editorial director, Miriam Hodgson, said she had sometimes encouraged a writer of promising teenage stories to think in terms of a novel, pointing out that there were more openings in this field. Admitting she was a great believer in short stories, she suggested that unknown writers might find a way into the market by linking several tales together with a common background or theme, perhaps, or by bringing a few of the same characters into all of them.

If you feel you'd gain valuable practice and confidence by writing short stories, look upon them realistically as work which may be published in book form, if not at once, perhaps at some future stage of your career. Alternatively, consider the possibility of writing magazine fiction (discussed later on in this chapter) for which there is, on the whole, a greater demand. Remember, though, that the situation is changing all the time; at least one 'teens' journal has closed since I began planning this book, and others are changing direction, sometimes cutting down on their fiction content. There may well be more scope, over the next few years, for books of short stories. So, however many times your work is rejected, *don't tear it up*. Tuck it away safely, forget it for now and start writing something else. In two or three years' time, who knows . . .?

Many successful writers of fiction disagree strongly with the general assumption that short stories are easier to write than novels. The truth is that *because* they are short (between one and three thousand words, as a rough guide) they have to be very tightly – and therefore expertly – written, and a great deal of thinking and pre-planning is essential.

Of course you'll find similarities when comparing teenage novels with short story collections: beginnings which arouse curiosity, grab and hold attention . . . conflict, suspense, mystery, humour . . . situations and expressions which will (with luck) stand the test of time . . . properly rounded, sometimes unexpected, endings.

Now let's consider some of the ways in which short stories *differ* from novels. Obviously they have to progress at a far less leisurely pace; there is little room for gradual build-up of characters, places and background, or passages of unnecessary chat. Dialogue still has a vital part to play, but it should never slow down the action and movement of the plot. A single snatch of cleverly composed conversation may be used to define personalities while pushing the story ahead – *at the same time* evoking feelings of sympathy, shock or amusement.

The general rules (discussed in Chapter Three) about tense and first or third person narrative still apply, although the present tense is a little more usual in short stories. Most of these are written from the point of view of one protagonist only, but if two characters have their say, the change of viewpoint has to be made quite clear – possibly by use of sub-headings or a one-line break in the narrative.

Never lose sight of the fact that young people expect the near-impossibility of a strong and/or intriguing plot which is fairly easy to follow at every stage of its development.

Plot-building

Don't concern yourself too much with people who tell you there are only four – or five or three – basic plots. Rarely storytellers themselves, they may well be trying to wind you up, and their opinions are either cynical or boringly clinical. Themes may be similar, but it is the way in which they are treated which brings interest and individuality to what might seem at first to be an over-used plot.

Short story writers, like novelists, are often asked how they find their ideas, but, here again, there is no magic formula. Some authors like to create the characters first, developing their personalities and weaving a story around them. Others concentrate on some everyday situation – a mis-dialled telephone call, for instance, or a chance meeting in a dentist's waiting-room – and *continue* concentrating until a story begins to take form. Newspaper articles and readers' letter and problem pages are well known sources of inspiration. Many writers talk of the way plot ideas often spring to mind right out of the blue, and emphasize the importance of jotting them down, there and then, for future reference.

Short story collections – learning as you read

Once again, I must stress the value of studying the work of established authors, comparing plots and construction. You'll find that most of the collections on the young adult shelves have been written for the 11–14–year-olds who still enjoy books written specifically for their age group.

One notable exception is *A Walk on the Wild Side* by acclaimed novelist, Robert Westall, a fascinating collection of cat stories, 'guaranteed', as the blurb rightly claims, 'to frighten, amaze, chill and move.' Perusing this, with its grim settings – a World War II airfield in the wastes of Lincolnshire, for instance, and a bleak, windswept East coast seafront – I found myself forgetting that this anthology had been written with young adults in mind, although the plots were uncomplicated and the conclusions properly convincing. It was a book, I thought, that a parent might buy for a teenage son or daughter, with every intention of reading it themselves in due course.

In *A Ghostly Gathering*, Kenneth Ireland has written 13 'terrifying tales' for younger teenagers – though in spite of this blurbal warning, a few of them begin on a deceptively normal note: in one, a cheeky schoolboy is in every day trouble with a tetchy teacher, and another starts off innocently enough with a few kids planning a half-term camping expedition. In the final story, *The Door in the Wall*, the spookiness is there from the very first sentence.

> Sheila sensed there was something odd the moment she began to walk along Warren Lane. She had a sudden feeling that there were people around her, to such an extent that she actually began to look for them.

Several of the ghost stories in another collection, *One Step Beyond*, have lighthearted beginnings, but author Pete Johnson has given each of his tales a title page, with a few chilly introductory lines, such as these from *Secret Terror:*

> It had been Clare's worst fear. But she was older now, hadn't mentioned it for years. It was still there but only around the edges of her life.
>
> One day soon Clare hopes she will wake up and find it's disappeared for ever. But instead, she wakes up to discover her nightmare waiting there for her – and you.

The Mandarin 'Teens' series of short story collections (all edited by Miriam Hodgson) is worth studying, partly for the sheer variety of content, but also because at the back of each book is a fact-file section introducing the specially commissioned authors, recording their comments on writing and themselves.

One of these paperbacks, *Take Your Knee off my Heart*, contains nine love stories: very different, essentially readable tales, with intriguing openings and satisfying endings (whether happy, sad, amusing or unexpected). The writers were quite clearly aware that, in common with younger children, readers aged 11 and over expected properly rounded plots, a fair sprinkling of humour and/or excitement, and at least some characters with whom they could identify. I've chosen a few extracts as a way of illustrating the varying style and technique of some of the authors. First, Jenny Nimmo's opening paragraph in the title story:

> I was fifteen and had never been kissed, unless you count the exploratory fumblings of various unremarkable boys on various unremarkable school trips. A change of air always seems to bring it out in boys.

From these few sentences we learn that the narrator is a girl with a fairly streetwise attitude to life. This story, we suspect, in keeping with its title, will be a lighthearted romance, with neither moonlight-and-roses passion nor irreparably broken hearts. There is, nevertheless, a certain warmth in the ending:

> 'Look at me,' he demanded. I was. He looked wonderfully wartorn, with blackened cheeks and a purple eye, with a soot-stained shirt and bandaged hands. 'I've been beaten by your brother,' he said, 'bitten by your dog and burnt by your little sister's bungling. But I'm still here, aren't I? Wouldn't you call that love?'
>
> I couldn't deny it. I couldn't speak, in fact, because the next moment he was kissing me.
>
> And it was all that I'd dreamt of. Better actually!

While many popular crime and mystery novels have their moments of fun, there may be little room for humour in short story thrillers, where amusing repartee might merely detract from the overall feel of suspense. The tense, uneasy mood throughout another of these love stories – *Santa Caterina*, by Anthony Masters – is apparent from the very beginning:

> If only we'd never gone there, thought Alan. They were scrambling up the mountainside in the late afternoon heat. Alice was so tanned that she looked as if she had lived on the Mediterranean for months, while he, being fair, had turned a blotchy, peeling red.
>
> He looked up at the bare mountainside, the path twisting upwards towards the cairn cross, the white heat bleaching the rock. Why on earth couldn't they talk about it? Why couldn't he even accuse her?

Finally, I must mention Mary Hooper's contribution to this particular 'Teens' collection: *A Morning in the Life . . .* Stories written in the intimate form of a diary are well known to be popular with young readers (think of Adrian Mole) and in this case the narrator is a schoolgirl called Hannah, who begins her 5-hour saga without preamble, merely stating the time of day:

> 7.00 a.m.
> The alarm goes off and I spring out of bed just like they do in the commericals for cornflakes. It is the last day of term, a beautiful sunny day and also positively the last day for getting off with Luke Sanders so I have certain things to do.

Note the confidential tone in that opening passage and how the sense of immediacy is strengthed by the almost breathless use of the present tense. As Hannah continues in this fashion, her personality is revealed by way of talk of her predicament and her deadly rival, the cleavage-showing, mini-skirted Lauren Kemp.

The writer makes further use of sub-headings to indicate the passing hours: 8.00 a.m., 9.00 a.m., 11.00 a.m. – ('break time') – thus ensuring that nothing interrupts the flow and pace of Hannah's morning, which reaches its climax at 1.00 p.m., when 'The rugby team, red in the face and looking sheepish, come into the cookery room.'

A story of this kind *has* to have a cheerful ending, and any attempt to moralize would be ridiculously superfluous, killing its devil-may-care charm stone dead. Here's how Mary Hooper concluded Hannah's tale:

> . . . and we both laugh – *just* as Lauren Kemp pushes past us with her cleavage heaving. It almost looks as if we're laughing at her and I don't do anything to correct the impression. She passes on, Luke pops another sugar slug into his mouth and . . . yes, I'm definitely feeling good about myself again.

Also worth perusal are the anthologies of short stories in the Puffin 'Plus' teenage series. In one of these, *Landmarks*, editor Nadia Wheatley has chosen nine tales 'set against a variety of rural and urban Australian landscapes, raising issues of friendship and sexuality, independence and integrity, and even the thin line between the real and imagined.'

Mightier than the Lipstick, another Puffin 'Plus', is a collection of short stories by different women writers, and has a distinctly adult feel about it. In the preface, editor Sue Adler writes:

> I chose the stories here primarily for the strength of their writing – the power of the pen – and their exceptional portrayal of women and women's lives in the contemporary world . . . Although there is far more literature by and about women published now as compared with the almost all-male cast of books I read as a teenager, there is still not enough – I'd like to see 51 per cent of the books on the shelves by, and about, women.

In the final short story in this collection, author Clodagh Corcoran takes an intriguingly unconventional view of the relationship between Snow White and the seven dwarfs. This set me thinking about the undercurrents of sexism present in most traditional fairy tales, and about the possibility of plots galore lurking innocently on nursery bookshelves, in need of no more than a little clever up-dating. (Easier said than done, you may say, but worth some thought, all the same.)

Stories with a sporting background remain as popular as ever, but it's no longer a matter of pony adventures for girls and football and cricket yarns for boys. There is a markedly unisex feel to the cover illustration of *A Sporting Chance*, compiled for The Bodley Head by novelist and playwright, Aidan Chambers, in which the blurb reveals, 'eight of his favourite authors for young readers tell stories . . . which are not so much about sport as they are about the people who take part.'

Those final words conjure up thoughts of well worn but favourite writing adage: 'A story is only as good as its characters.' It makes sense, on the whole, *particularly* in the case of short stories for young readers.

Submitting short stories to a publisher

In my view, 'Nothing venture, nothing gain' is another splendid proverb, and there's no reason why you shouldn't submit your stories to a publisher, provided you are willing to take a try-and-try-again approach.

To save unnecessary disappointment, scour the bookshop and library shelves for publishers with an obvious interest in teenage short story collections (assessing the age-groups covered) and check their details in *The Writer's Handbook* or *Writers' and Artists' Yearbook*. The rules of presentation and submitting are, in general, the same as those for novels (see Chapter Three) and if your stories have a central theme, mention this in your brief covering letter. Don't forget to include a stamped addressed envelope – *and be sure to keep copies of all stories sent*.

If your work is rejected, remember that you are trying to break into an extremely difficult market – and if you receive a few words of encouragement, feel very heartened indeed.

MAGAZINE FICTION

Of course there is a splendid kudos about writing books, but never feel there need be anything second-rate about magazine fiction and the people who write it. True, you may have to put up with non-writing friends' sniggery remarks about adults who 'churn out' romances for teenage journals – I've been through this myself and, yes, it's infuriating – but you'll find that professional writers take an entirely different attitude, knowing that unless work shows talent, it is unlikely to sell *anywhere*.

Publishers tend to show a keener interest in a novel written by someone who has already sold magazine fiction – and this I've learned through personal experience. It was because I'd written countless stories and serials for teenage weeklies that I was commissioned, on the strength of two chapters and a synopsis, to write my first young adult novel. Mainly thanks to all the picture story scripts I'd sold when my daughters were small, I was invited, by a producer, to write one of a series of half-hour TV plays for older schoolchildren. Times are tougher now and, in both these instances, luck played its part – but then it always does.

Many published novelists continue to write magazine stories – for money, for practice and for fun – and as one author said, 'They're something to get on with during the endless wait for a publisher's verdict on a book idea.'

At one time it was possible to make a living out of writing teenage magazine fiction, but several publications have closed recently, resulting in far fiercer competition; even so, there is still a market for promising material. Payment varies from paper to paper and is made on acceptance or publication, and in some cases is surprisingly good. If you have the necessary ability as a storyteller and are prepared to tailor your work to the needs of different editors, you may well find yourself earning some useful extra income in a very enjoyable way.

Exploring the market

It would be impossible to overemphasize the importance of studying a magazine before submitting a story to the fiction editor. With teenage journals in particular, unsuitable material is one of the main reasons for the rejection of work by competent writers. A story may be too young or too old in outlook, the style may be too simple, condescending or quirky, the theme inappropriate. With a little careful investigation, new writers will avoid this surprisingly common cause of disappointment.

Through surveys and other market research, each magazine editor builds up a fairly clear picture of her 'average' reader: age, interests, likes and dislikes. With this in mind, she develops the policy of her magazine, and chooses its contents accordingly. I broached the subject with several editors and their advice was unanimous: *read the magazine first*.

In the present climate of uncertainty – with rumoured threats of closures and vague talk of new titles appearing to fill gaps in the market – I feel it would be unhelpful to be overly specific when discussing the fiction requirements of the various teenage magazines in circulation at the time of writing. You'll find more information about these in the current edition of *The Magazine Writer's Handbook*, but as author Gordon Wells admits in his introduction: 'Any handbook such as this is almost bound to be out of date in some details before it can be published.'

The only safe approach is to keep a watchful eye on the magazine racks, perhaps in supermarkets and big stationers such as W.H. Smith, where customers can and do browse at will, feeling under no pressure to purchase. It pays, neverthless, to be on friendly terms with your local newsagent, who may be able to give you advance information on new publications.

Glance at the 'contents' pages of young adult magazines and buy any which contain fiction. Take these home and study them critically for the type and length of stories – and read the features, agony columns and letters to the editor for ideas – and build up your own picture of that all-important 'average' reader.

You may like to submit a story right away, or alternatively – and perhaps more sensibly – write to the fiction editor of your chosen magazine, enquiring if she or he accepts stories from freelance writers and also asking about the availability of a guidelines leaflet. Make your letter brief and to the point, and enclose a stamped addressed envelope. If you decide to request guidelines from more than one editor, resist the temptation to send copies of the same story to several publications, which, apart from being unprofessional, might well lead to embarrassment and confusion later on. If and when your work is rejected, by all means submit it to another magazine, but some revision may be necessary, to fit in with a different editorial policy.

Fiction guidelines

Because magazine offices tend to be swamped with unsolicited manuscripts, many of them regrettably unsuitable, it has become quite usual for a fiction editor to prepare a page or two of information about the kind of stories she (or he) is looking for. These guidelines can be of tremendous value to would-be writers, enabling them to study the relevant magazine in a much more analytical way.

Just Seventeen is one of the few young-adult journals to have grown in popularity in spite of the recession. Fiction editor, Jacqui Deevoy, sent me a copy of her current style sheet, and the following extract will give you an idea of just *how* helpful a leaflet of this kind can be.

WHO YOU ARE WRITING FOR

The typical JUST SEVENTEEN reader is:

1. Female
2. 14 years old
3. At school
4. Not an avid fiction reader although she may read the occupational blockbuster and short stories in other magazines.

THE STORIES

All stories should contain:

1. A strong hook, as near to the beginning as possible
2. 'Action' appearing early in the story to draw reader in

3. Situations which a 14-year-old reader can either identify with or aspire to

All stories should have:
1. A strong storyline
2. A reasonable amount of dialogue
3. An interesting twist at the end
4. Not too many unnecessary characters – all characters (and events) should be relevant to the plot

These guidelines continue with more details of the stories themselves, the advised length and hints on presentation, plus information on matters of payment and the editor's and authors' rights. By the time this book is published, the requirements may have changed, but to receive a current copy, send your request in writing to the fiction editor (enclosing s.a.e.).

The same procedure applies if you'd like guideline sheets from other magazines; check the addresses and names of fiction editors in the journals themselves or from current copies of writers' yearbooks. Much can be learned from comparing one leaflet with another, and all the ones I've read mention the age group to aim for, and the importance of strong story lines and intriguing openings.

Loving Monthly publishes over fifteen short stories per issue, but has changed dramatically since its days as a weekly magazine for schoolgirl devotees of love-and-kisses teenage romance. It is now targeted at an older readership (18-plus) and many of the stories have an undisguisedly erotic flavour, although care is taken in both fiction and features to stress the dangers of casual promiscuity. The guidelines suggest a need for 'Mills & Boon-style passion' and stories which are 'erotic but not too explicit (definitely no four-letter-words!)' Also mentioned are hospital sagas and tales of the supernatural, '. . . anything, provided romance, whether happy or tragic, is the main ingredient.' Again, I strongly advise careful study of an up-to-date copy of the guidelines and, of course, the magazine itself.

The flashback technique

If, as advised by so many editors, you start your own short story at a point of high drama, you may be faced with the need, sooner rather than later, to explain the events which led up to this carefully chosen moment of excitement. Here the flashback technique is often very effective, though some writing tutors insist (rightly, I think) that it should be used sparingly and with caution.

The rules are quite simple, and involve the use of the pluperfect tense. By way of explanation, I've concocted these few opening lines of an imaginary teenage story:

> 'So it was you!' I yelled, thrusting the letter into Pete's hand. 'You're the troublemaker who invented those dire lies about that poor, lonely old woman.'
>
> Ignoring his protests, I stormed off down the street, wondering what on earth I'd ever seen in such a pathetic creep. And yet just ten days ago, Pete Lee had fooled me into thinking he was a nice, straightforward guy.
>
> I remembered the cheerful way he'd offered to help me to deliver the sports club magazines. 'It'll take you half the night on your own,' he'd said, all mock concern. 'Why don't we do it together, Liz?'
>
> I'd shrugged, trying not to look as pleased as I felt. 'OK, I said. 'Let's go.'
>
> We talked about this and that as we set off towards the club . . .

Here, I used the pluperfect tense to move the story back to its true beginning – '*had* fooled me' . . . '*he'd* said' – but slid back into the normal past tense a few sentences later, to avoid the unnatural-sounding clumsiness of continued use of the pluperfect.

The story would then carry on in the past tense, leading up to the point where Liz yells at Pete. At this stage, the pluperfect might be used again, but even more briefly:

> That's when I'd yelled at him, thrusting the letter into his hand before storming off down the street. I thought I heard him shouting my name, but I didn't look back.

When reading novels and short stories watch out for the various ways in which other writers make use of flashbacks. With practice, and treated carefully, it's a very convenient trick of the trade.

Dialogue in magazine fiction

Although the sections on dialogue (beginning on page 38) may be helpful in general, a rather different approach should be given to the question of jargon in teenage magazines.

For a start, you needn't worry about using ultra-trendy 'in' words, for fear of their sounding dated this time next year. While a novel or book of stories may be expected to live on for a decade or more, a magazine is itself dated after a week or a month, when a new issue takes its place. So forget the future and concentrate on the here and now; the more up-to-date your jargon, the better for you and everyone else concerned.

Consider these few words of advice, taken from one editor's 3-page set of guidelines for writers:

> . . . many otherwise good stories are spoilt by old-fashioned language and descriptions such as a girl putting on a stole to go out in the evening, or expressions from the Sixties, such as 'groovy'! Do watch TV, keep your ears open in public and catch the flavour of today's vocabulary.

Again, it's worth finding ways of meeting and talking to young people, but you'll be helped almost as much by taking note of the jargon used in squeaky-new issues of teenage magazines – particularly the one you are trying to write for.

Stories with a twist

Every one of the fiction editors I interviewed mentioned the popularity among young readers of short-short stories (1,000 words or perhaps even less) with unexpected endings. You'll find examples galore when studying magazine fiction – and the reading or re-reading of Roald Dahl's renowned 'twist-in-tale' collections for adults will teach a valuable lesson in itself (a highly enjoyable one, at that).

'Twists' are not easy to write because unless the endings come as a total surprise, the stories fall dismally flat. After completing one, I usually ask a good friend or my daughter to read it, afterwards asking when he or she guessed how it would end; this way I discover whether I've given too much away too soon. Some clues are vital, but I find it hard to gauge on my own how many are needed to create the right and sometimes almost teasing atmosphere of suspense.

Because my memory is fickle, I find it necessary, too, to scribble town 'twist' ideas the moment they spring to mind. I once scrawled the bare bones of a plot onto the back of my hand while queueing in my local supermarket, which no doubt caused a few startled glances from other shoppers.

Magazine serials

Some teenage magazines run regular or occasional serials (i.e. longer stories divided into 2, 3, or more parts) but these are nearly always commissioned by fiction editors who will almost certainly advise new writers to concentrate on getting a few short stories accepted first. In spite of their length, serials are in some ways less time-consuming to work on: there's just one plot to devise, one set of characters . . .

If you are interested, the chapters on novel-writing may help – and you should always submit a synopsis first – but here's another tip, learned through grim experience, which you may find useful. Set aside a notebook for the serial you are working on; in it jot down characters' names, brief notes about them, and the happenings in the story – dates, places, etc. By doing this you'll avoid the hassle, as your work progresses, of having to search through reams of copy whenever you feel unsure of facts and conversation featured in earlier episodes.

Science fiction

You will no doubt have discovered that most teenage magazines are aimed at girls, although a fair proportion of the fiction content is written by men, and some of the stories are told from a male point of view.

Tales of fantasy are highly popular at present, and many teenagers of both sexes enjoy science fiction magazines, although most of these are written for enthusiasts of all ages.

While investigating openings for freelancers, I spoke to Julian Flood, who has been writing and selling science fiction for some years now and claims, rather intriguingly, that a SF writer 'is a bit like an Old Testament prophet.'

Payment is rarely astonishingly high, but for anyone keen to break into the market, here are some extracts from Julian's lighthearted but helpful notes on the subject:

> Science fiction spawns a lot of very short-lived magazines; they come in with a fanfare, push out a few issues, and go bust – usually just after saying they want one of my stories. . .
>
> SF has changed since the really famous writers (Heinlen, Asimov, Clarke) were active. The only way you can find out which planet the genre currently orbits is by reading the magazines and books – not just those found in W.H. Smith

(e.g. *Interzone: Science Fiction and Fantasy*) but the American ones, too. Find out where they can be bought/obtained by joining the British Science Fiction Association, which reviews and publicizes them. (Address enquiries to: The Membership Secretary, 29 Thornville Road, Hartlepool, Cleveland TS26 8EW)

Writing photostory scripts

In the Eighties, photostory papers were highly popular with teenage and younger girls scriptwriters were in great demand and reasonably well paid. Because of closures there are fewer openings now, though as the economic climate improves, there may well be a revival of interest.

The construction of a photostory is similar to that of a play, and if you are considering the idea of writing drama, script-writing will provide useful practice in story-telling by way of dialogue.

Keep a lookout for photostory papers, new and established. Buy and study one or more and write a brief letter to the fiction editor (enclosing s.a.e.) asking if he or she accepts work from freelance writers and if they have guidelines. When reading these stories, note how the plot develops from frame to frame with speech and 'thinks' bubbles, and brief captions which move the action ahead. As well as the ability to devise entertaining but tightly written dialogue, scriptwriters must also have a certain visual knack which enables them to 'see' in their minds the scenes they are creating. These they have to describe, in brief note form, to magazine photographers.

From the papers themselves, you'll discover the types of stories required, style, length and so on. The following few frames will give you an idea of layout. (Double spacing is always used, to allow for editorial notes and corrections.)

---

1. In school grounds, Viv runs excitedly up to curious Kim. Both girls and any pupils in background wear uniform.

PANEL: One morning at break. . .

VIV: KIM – YOU'RE NOT GOING TO BELIEVE THIS –

KIM: DON'T TELL ME – PHIL LODGE HAS TAKEN UP KNITTING!

---

2. Closer view of Viv's and Kim's intrigued faces.

VIV: NOTHING AS TAME AS THAT. FACT IS, HE'S TAKEN UP WITH SHARON CARR.

KIM: SHY MOUSE SHARON? YOU DON'T MEAN IT, VIV – YOU'RE WINDING ME UP!

---

3. Walking with Kim towards school entrance, Viv points to Sharon and Phil, standing together, talking earnestly.

VIV: MARIE SPOTTED THEM IN THE PARK YESTERDAY, HOLDING HANDS . . . AND DON'T LOOK NOW, BUT THERE THEY ARE TOGETHER –

KIM: SO IT'S TRUE! BUT PHIL'S SUCH A HUNK . . . WHAT CAN HE POSSIBLY SEE IN SHARON?

---

4. In a classroom, Kim sits dismally at her desk, clearly paying no attention to the lesson.

PANEL: Later . . .

VIV (thinks): I'M SO SHATTERED, I CAN'T CONCENTRATE ON HISTORY OR ANYTHING ELSE . . . JUST WHEN I THOUGHT PHIL WAS BEGINNING TO SHOW AN INTEREST IN *ME*! I'VE GOTTA DO SOMETHING ABOUT THIS – BUT WHAT?

Scripting picture stories

A few teenagers still enjoy picture-story papers (*Bunty*, for example) and, in some ways, these are easier than photostories to compile, although the layout is similar. Because the frame-by-frame scenes are drawn by artists, writers are less restricted – by the cost of exotic settings, for instance, and too many characters. Where a photographic model would be unlikely to agree to be pushed, fully dressed, into a river, or to fall off a cliff, pen-and-brush characters can get up to just about anything.

Once you've learned the technique, you may thoroughly enjoy writing story-by-dialogue scripts, and if an editor shows interest in your work, you have good reason to celebrate.

The editor's decision

Don't be put off by people who shake their heads knowingly, saying that editors pay little or no attention to the unsolicited manuscripts piled up in their trays. This may have been true, to some extent, forty years ago but nowadays it is simply *not* the case.

I have worked for and on teenage magazines for many years, and I assure you that fiction editors take great pleasure – glee in exceptional circumstances – in discovering talented new authors. Once a writer has sold a few good stories, meetings are often arranged to discuss plots, serials and material for annual fiction supplements. Editors know that everyone benefits from a good, friendly relationship between a magazine's staff and its regular writers.

Fiction editors, however, are busy people, often putting in long hours, and they can't be blamed for spending little time on the work of unknown writers who quite obviously haven't bothered to study the story content of their magazines. They are similarly put off by poor presentation, clumsy style and faulty grammar (see Chapter Seven).

There is little hope for Christmas stories submitted in late November, simply because magazine staff work weeks or even months in advance, and will have put their December issues together earlier in the autumn. (Stockpiling is rare, these days.) Tales of gloom and despondency (about AIDS, say, and near-death experiences) are also discouraged. Says Jacqui Deevoy of *Just Seventeen*: 'We are inundated with such stories and very few of them are original enough to be appealing.'

Careless inaccuracies lead to rejections, too. Often short-staffed, editors are understandably wary of writers who can't be relied upon to do their own research before submitting stories. Consider these words of warning from one editor's guidelines: 'A simple blunder such as having people counting their pesetas in Greece, or tenderly whispering 'Mon amour . . .' in Italy, will lead us to suspect that there are errors in the rest of the story, too.'

Submitting magazine stories – a checklist

You may find it helpful to refer to the notes on professional presentation given in Chapter Three, but here are the basic, accepted rules of submitting a story to a magazine fiction editor:

- Work should be typed in double spacing on one side only of fairly good quality A4 paper. Last-minute corrections should be neat, legible and kept to a minimum. Number the pages and make sure the manuscript is clean and fresh in appearance.

- Secure the pages with a paper-clip or stapler, and attach a title sheet on which you have typed (top left), 'Short Story' and the approximate length. The title of the story should be centred halfway down the page, with your name or pseudonym below it. Your real name and address should appear both at the foot of this and the last page of the manuscript.

- Enclose a very brief covering letter and a stamped addressed envelope of adequate size for the return of your work. As always make sure you have a copy of your own.

- Be prepared for a fairly long wait and resist the temptation to make telephone enquiries.

Note: Payment for magazine stories is made either on acceptance or publication. Some writers type 'FBSR' on title sheets, indicating that they are offering first British serial rights only (in the hope of selling second serial rights at some future date) but rights are usually negotiated by editors at the time of acceptance. A few magazine publishers insist on buying all rights, and may then re-use a piece of work as often as they please, without any further payment to the author.

5
Non-fiction: books and magazine features

Successful writers of teenage non-fiction often have to be as imaginative in their writing as novelists and other storytellers. On the whole, publishers and magazine editors are looking not only for expert knowledge, but also for infectious enthusiasm, originality and a deceptively easy style which simultaneously informs and entertains. Of course many non-fiction books and articles are written merely to amuse, and if you have a natural ability to make people laugh, you'll find it well worth working on this, because talented humorists are few and far betweem.

While you should accept that many teenagers head straight for the adult book and magazine shelves when searching for information, you may find some consolation from the fact that adults, when taking up a new interest – photography, say, or the game of bridge – frequently prefer the step-by-step simplicity of 'young adult' instruction books.

NON-FICTION BOOKS

The majority of information books are written by experts in their fields and their qualifications and achievements are usually featured on the covers, to promote sales. Editors of encyclopedic volumes – on the history of sport or music, say – tend to commission teams of writers highly specialized in the subjects covered. Anyone who wishes (and is academically equipped) to contribute to works of this kind should, as a possible first move, send background details and examples of his or her work to carefully selected publishers.

If you feel you are adequately qualified to write a book on your craft, profession, hobby or whatever, take a look at some of the non-fiction works for older schoolchildren currently on sale, and note how they differ from books for adults and younger readers on similar subjects. Compare methods of approach – of hooking and holding interest – and ways of blending friendly humour into passages of easy-to-follow instruction.

Of course you'll find information-only books, many of them compiled by just one author, where humour plays little part, and handbooks of this kind are usually aimed at young people less interested in leisurely reading than in finding out facts – on their rights as teenagers, for instance, or spare-time activities. These manuals often contain a mass of painstakingly researched material, carefully sectioned, with notes on further reading and addresses of relevant associations and clubs.

Young people, like many adults, seem fascinated by celebrities, TV and pop stars, sporting personalities, but biographies of such people are usually written by specially commissioned authors. 'Star' autobiographies are often, but not always, ghosted by professional writers, whose names may appear on front covers, usually in fairly small print. Neither publishers nor the stars themselves are likely to consider unestablished writers for this kind of work, but you may be in with a chance if the personality happens to be, say, a close friend since schooldays. Would-be biographers might be better advised to think in terms of historical characters of particular interest to young people, perhaps linking some of them together, by way of a common cause or outlook. (Remember always that to schoolchildren anything pre – 1970 is 'history'.)

I have already stressed the value, to researchers, of visiting libraries and bookshops at off-peak times, when staff members are freer to answer questions and discuss the more popular books on their shelves. A glance at the date stamps in library books will give you an idea of how frequently they are borrowed, helping you to assess popularity by yourself, but pay particular attention to more recently published works.

Here are some titles to look out for, which may be of help when you are deciding on the subject matter and structure of a non-fiction book of your own. When considering how well any illustrations complement the text, bear in mind that publishers often prefer to do their own commissioning of artists and photgraphers. (More details on page 75)

Check Out Chess by Bob Wade and Ted Nottingham is an attractively presented paperback picked from the wide range of modern 'how-to' books for young adults. Although the authors are well-known and highly regarded in the austere world of chess, there is nothing starchy in the way in which the whys and wherefores of the game – rules, moves, ploys – are put across. The instructions and diagrams are clear and to the point, but there's an abundance of between-lesson fun, with cartoons and informal chat. The book opens with the story of how a game once stopped a famous battle, and the text quickly moves on to explain why chess itself is a 'war game'. (And that is enough in itself to incite many younger readers to press on.)

Zany Jewellery is another mix of instruction and fun. The cover claims boldly that everything is cheap and easy to make, and writer Juliet Bawden has clearly enjoyed bringing an old-fashioned craft right up to date, with nicely flip headings, such as 'Putting on the Glitz'. Very important in a book of this kind, she has also taken care to give details of where to buy or scavenge for the materials needed.

Teenagers worry about appearances perhaps even more than most people and *How do I look?* is a particularly good example of the way a book can be made up largely of interviews with unknown people who have strong, sometimes conflicting, opinions on a single topic of interest. In this case, Jill Dawson (described up front as poet, freelance writer and editor) has invited several girls and young women to 'talk about how they feel about their changing bodies, dressing to make a statement, challenging stereotypes.' These interviewees are referred to by Christian name only, with admirably professional and emotive photographs by Sally Feldt.

Countless readers will identify with Janet, who wants people to notice her, but this is not a frivolous book, and the humour is more often wry than hilarious. Take, for instance, these reflections by Hannah on pressures and the way 'people judge you by the way you look'. . .

> Even my dad, he makes sexist remarks about my looks. He's a sexist jerk, anyway, I've never lived with him. He thinks all women should look like Page 3 models, so he always comments on my short haircut, clumpy shoes, 'man's' coat, etc . . . Luckily I only see him one to three times a year – when I need money, usually.

Note the feel of compassion always present in this book, and how the talks on obsessions, anorexia among them, conclude with a section on how to get help.

Relationships and other problems

While reasearching, you'll almost certainly find evidence of a growing demand for books on adolescent relationships. Variations abound on the themes of sexual know-how and boy-girl encounters, most of them pleasingly wholesome, whether serious or funny, although I found one or two rather tackily facetious. By no means all these books are targeted only at girls; it's actually recognized nowadays that boys have problems, too.

One I recommend, partly for its insight into the ways and lifestyle of younger teenagers, is *Boys about Boys*, subtitled 'The facts, fears and fantasies'. A further cunning coverline makes this bold claim: 'Essential reading for all boys – *and* girls!'

Author Nick Fisher is the popular, resident agony uncle on *Just Seventeen* magazine and this paperback might aptly be described as a book-length problem page. In it he discusses and answers queries from boys (e.g. Leroy, 14) and a few girls, too, about familiar adolescent hassles, ranging from shyness to 'popular myths about contraception'. All in all, it's a splendid book; the information and opinions are sound and the warnings friendly but clear. I can almost hear some reader's mother sighing over it with her husband, saying, 'If only there'd been something like this when *we* were young.'

In his introduction, and with far less squidgy sentimentality, Nick Fisher remembers his schoolmates' hair-raising attempts to become sexually aware, and his own solution to what was, in those days, an embarrassingly pressing problem.

> I was lucky. I had access to three vital sources of information: sisters, sisters' friends and sisters' magazines. I started reading the features and problem pages of my sisters' *Jackie* and *Petticoat* magazines and soon learnt that there was an awful lot that the big boys behind the Portakabin didn't know.

Less an informal chat session, more a straightforward information manual, *Loving Encounters* by Rosemary Stones is captioned in characteristically matter-of-fact terms, as 'A book for teenagers about sex'. Covering a wide range of topics, including gay relationships, AIDS and rape, it has been praised by the *Times Educational Supplement* for stressing throughout the importance of '. . . loving, sharing and enjoyment'.

If you have appropriate experience – as a counsellor or psychologist, say, or a working member of a youth organization – and would like to tackle of book of this kind, try to devise an original treatment as a way of persuading publishers that your book will stand out from the rest.

Peter Corey and Kara May have given intriguing novelty value to their recent, highly popular handbook, *Coping with Girls/Coping with Boys*, which is instantly recognizable as two separate volumes in one: double-fronted and enabling readers, after consulting the boys' section, to turn it upside down and plunge into the girls' half, as if starting an entirely new book.

Information books: finding a new angle

Even if your chosen subject is less noticeably in vogue, you may find it has already been covered in book form by other writers, in which case you should rack your brains for an imaginatively different angle when preparing an outline for a publisher. (And you should *always* submit an outline before spending weeks or months on a concept which may, for one reason or another, fail to attract interest. For more details, see page 77.)

Bear in mind that teenagers are notoriously short of money and will usually welcome information on entertaining leisure-time activities which cost next-to-nothing. By all means look for new slants on traditional games and puzzles, but *new* must always be the operative word, as the market is swamped with books of braintwisters, conjuring tricks, wordsearches, and so on.

Computers – computer games, in particular – may be today's craze to end all crazes, but even electronic wizards will find difficulty in breaking into this fiercely competitive field. If you are an addict yourself, a study of relevant magazines and the contents of already overcrowded bookshelves will help you to assess whether you really have something original to contribute.

Humour can certainly encourage interest in subjects which

might otherwise be considered unlikely to be of instant appeal to less scholarly young adults. John Farman has injected a continuous flow of fun into *The Very Bloody History of England*.

In some ways, this might be compared to the Thirties classic, *1066 and All That*, but Farman's book is Nineties through and through. In my opinion it's a clever and valuable aid to learning; there for the taking are the genuine facts – some of which, surely, will be effortlessly absorbed even by readers mainly concerned with the surrounding joviality.

The pen-and-ink drawings, most of them in comic-cartoon style, have been drawn by the author, who sets the mood with a cover illustration of a ye olde helmeted soldier peeping over castle battlements, announcing in his speech bubble that here is history 'without the boring bits'. In spite of this claim, a tremendous amount of knowledge has been crammed in. Subheadings, particularly necessary in information books for young readers, add pace and zest to the passing of time. This snippet will give you a taste of the overall mix of fact and fun:

> 1610 – Distant Lands
> James personally hated the Puritans and finally lost his rag and told them that if they didn't conform to the Anglican church they could jolly well get lost. They took the hint and set out in a boat called the *Mayflower* to try to find Virginia. They got a bit lost, but did find America. Rather cheekily, they named the bit that they eventually landed on, New England (which it still is).

Clearly, 'supernatural' books are in great demand and 21,000 copies of Kenneth Ireland's *True Ghost Stories* have already been sold in Australia alone. Interestingly, it has been discovered that this collection is enjoyed by adults as well as the older schoolchildren for whom it was originally intended.

Hints for non-specialist writers

When interviewing Kenneth Ireland, a one-time teacher and now a prolific and enviably successful writer of novels, non-fiction and school textbooks for younger teenagers, I was interested to hear him stress more than once that he had no formal qualifications for writing any of his information books. 'I find most of the necessary facts from libraries,' he said, 'along with a certain amount of pleasurable delving, here and there.'

Endearingly, he seemed genuinely amazed by the success of his first non-fiction book, *Who Invented, Discovered, Made the First*? Published originally in 1988, this he has now revised, under the slicker title of *Who Invented the First?*, as the opener of a new series of books, all written by him.

'Series are something worth working on, as a long-term project,' he said, mentioning two follow-up titles: *Unsolved Mysteries* and *The Book of Discoveries*. 'After enjoying one of a series, a reader will look out for others.'

I asked Kenneth for some hints for new writers of non-fiction, and here are a few of the points he made . . .

- When mulling over possible themes, try to find a gap in the market. If there's not a clear gap, do *better* than what already exists.

- Whatever you're working on, keep your eyes and ears open for ideas which may fit into future projects. Snip bits out of newspapers which may, one day, fit something or other you have vaguely in mind. (I keep mine in a box.)

- If you are a teacher and find that you and your pupils are dissatisfied with a textbook, consider the idea of writing a more appealing one yourself. Submit your suggestion, a carefully planned synopsis and sample chapter to a publisher of textbooks used by your own or other classes. True, these are not the world's greatest money-spinners, but they are a way of getting yourself established as an author.

- If you enjoy what you are doing, this will show in your books. When tackling non-fiction, you are more often than not setting yourself up as a writer and researcher in one, and the work can be gruellingly hard. If it gives you no pleasure, pack it in, reminding yourself that there are other ways of making a living.

Research

Authors of non-fiction books often say that they find the research every bit as enjoyable as the actual writing. They also stress the importance of checking and re-checking facts, because even slight inaccuracies can do much to damage a writer's reputation, in the eyes of both publishers and those razor-sharp young readers who take wicked pleasure in pointing out blunders to their teachers, parents and mates.

By studying the 'Acknowledgements' sections of handbooks and manuals, you'll learn a lot about the ways and means other writers use when seeking and checking information on their chosen subjects. Firstly, I'd like to draw your attention to *Know Your Rights*, Sue Sharpe's excellent guide to under-18s on knowing where they stand 'in the many dilemmas of everyday life'. Among the subjects covered are the legal aspects of harassment at work, racial discrimination and indecent assault – and the author's awareness of the vital need for accuracy in such matters is made clear in her acknowlegements column, where she expresses her thanks to members of countless organizations, including the Children's Law Centre, the London University Institute of Education and the Belfast Law Centre.

If you are a librarian, with professional knowledge of research, you may already be thinking in terms of writing a book of this kind. Perhaps the most exciting I found was *Where to Join*: a guide to opportunities for young people, with special emphasis on outdoor adventure. In it are chapters on caving, climbing, pets, watersports – 'everything, according to the blurb, 'from airships to youth hostelling'. Each entry comes complete with details and addresses of the organizations concerned, cost of membership and so on. My mind boggles at the amount of work involved, but author Helen Pain, a university lecturer on Library Studies, was well qualified to take on such a mammoth task.

Because these books are crammed with information on topics of interest to teenagers, they may also be of valuable inspirational benefit to writers of both fact and fiction, magazine journalists included, anyone looking for new ideas.

If you are keen to look more deeply into the question of research, and information on such matters as indexing your book in due course, I strongly recommend a perusal of the recently revised edition of Ann Hoffmann's handbook, *Research for Writers*. (For more details, see page 113.)

Illustrations

I've always envied people talented enough to illustrate their own books, but have rarely come across them. Unless you are absolutely sure of your abilities as an artist or photographer, you'll probably find it safer to push all thoughts of illustrations to one side while working to interest a publisher in your idea.

Of course artwork of some kind may be necessary to your book – how-to-do-it diagrams, perhaps – but this is usually something to be discussed with publishers *after* they have shown the all-important initial interest. Even slightly inferior illustrations may have a damaging effect on an otherwise good proposal and, in any case, publishers often expect and prefer to choose their own artists.

If, on the other hand, you are working in partnership with a professional illustrator, on a book in which text and artwork are of equal importance, you will obviously need to submit samples of both when approaching a publisher. Just be very wary of enlisting the help of an amateur friend or relation at this crucial stage.

Submitting your proposal: points to consider

While studying the market you will no doubt have made a note of possible publishers, whose lists include books compatible with the one you intend to write. After making your first choice, think long and hard about how you'll go about convincing a commissioning editor that your idea is worth considering, and that you are more than capable of writing a book of this kind.

When I discussed the matter with Susie Gibbs, non-fiction editor of Pan Macmillan Children's Books, she offered this piece of advice:

> 'When gathering your information together – all of which must be of interest to young people – make sure you can sustain the idea for more than a brief synopsis.'

Allay any doubts you may have about this and anything else by preparing (for your own use, initially) a rough but fairly detailed chapter-by-chapter plan of your book, as you envisage it so far. If you find signs of sparsity in places, look for possible ways of adding substance, but firmly reject any thoughts of padding for padding's sake, which would almost certainly result in a tedious end-product.

Susie Gibbs and several other publishing editors agreed

that, as a first move, you should submit a synopsis of the proposed book, a sample chapter (of about 1,000 words) and a few brief notes on your background, including mention of previously published work – fiction included – and reasons why you feel qualified to write on your chosen subject.

When writing and revising a sample chapter, and it would seem sensible to make it Chapter One, bear in mind suggestions made earlier in this non-fiction section. Concentrate on hooking the reader, and make every paragraph play its part in retaining interest. The copy you submit to a publisher should, of course, be in double spacing on reasonably good quality A4 paper. (Most of the basic rules of presentation are the same as those given for novels, beginning on page 45.)

Next, the synopsis . . . An established author's outline may be fairly concise at this exploratory stage, but new writers should work on a more detailed synopsis. (There are no set rules on length, but think roughly in terms of two or three sheets of A4 paper and include your name and address and the working title of your book on the first page.) Take great care to prepare a professional proposal, giving a tightly written description of what you have on offer. Look on it, perhaps, as an advertising feature in which you are trying to sell your work and yourself, and make good use of your chapter-by-chapter plan. Give a clear idea of structure, sectioning and overall feel – let the publisher see that you know what you're about.

When tackling a serious theme – an information-only manual, for instance – you may decide to cut down a little on amusing asides, but do show enthusiasm for your subject where possible. If, on the other hand, yours is to be a lighthearted book, you may not find it easy to inject more than a few sparks of wit into this otherwise formal proposal; if you can, do – but don't go over the top.

I discussed the tricky question of illustrations earlier in this chapter, but when these form a vital part of your work, you will obviously wish to say so in your synopsis. When deciding whether or not to include a sample or two, tread very carefully if your writing is your main asset.

There's another small point worth considering. Now and again, in a work of non-fiction, you'll see mention on the jacket of a preface written by a well known authority on the subject covered. This can be a very good selling-aid, as I found out for myself when flipping through a book club catalogue, with little intention of buying anything. Then I noticed that P.D. James, my favourite crime novelist, had written the preface to Michael Legat's *Writing for Pleasure and Profit*. I immediately reached for the order form – and now recommend this splendidly helpful book to writers everywhere – but it was the P.D. James coverline which sold it to me. (If she approves, I'd thought, it must be worth having.)

So . . . if you're trying to sell a book on athletics and happen to be chummy enough with an international sprinter to persuade him or her to write your preface, mention this in your synopsis. It all sounds highly unlikely, I agree, but it *does* happen, from time to time.

Once you're happy with your synopsis, list your qualifications on a separate sheet, and again include your name and address. (If you've no formal headed A4 paper, you'll find personalized labels highly useful at a time like this.) Add details of published work, as suggested above, and any relevant background information.

Finally, write a brief covering letter, merely asking for your idea to be considered, and send everything off (with suitably sized s.a.e.) to your chosen publisher. Then prepare yourself for quite a long wait.

When a publisher shows interest

Don't listen to people, usually jokers, who claim that the real work doesn't begin until a publisher shows interest in your proposal. An unknown writer who reaches this indescribably exciting stage has undoubtedly put in a great deal of painstakingly hard slog already.

I mentioned earlier that, as a general rule, a first novel has to be completed before any serious talk of contracts is made. With a non-fiction book you may be offered a contract (and advance royalties) on the strength of your synopsis and sample chapter, although a publisher will very probably expect you to revise or add to these before coming to a decision. Persevere with any demands made, looking upon them as proof of the remarkable headway you've made so far.

Whether or not you decide to complete your book without a formal contract will possibly depend on your financial circumstances, and obviously you have the option of submitting your proposal to another publisher.

(Some of the points made in Chapters Three and Seven may be of help and interest while you are in the progress of writing and trying to sell your non-fiction work.)

MAGAZINE FEATURES

I have already mentioned the comings and goings of teenage journals and, sadly, over the last two or three years, I've seen rather more goings than comings, with rumours of magazine closures casting a shadow on the cheeriest of editorial offices.

For all that, there's still a demand for orginal feature ideas from editors of young adult periodicals. The first step, as always, is to make a study of the surviving 'teen mags' and keep a watchful eye on the shelves for new titles. Don't be deceived by the ostensibly adult air of some of the glossier publications; a scan of the 'contents' pages may reveal subject matter mainly of interest to the under-twenties, most of whom would be mortified if caught reading anything remotely resembling 'kids' stuff'.

Before beginning this section, I called into by nearest branch of W.H. Smith for a look at the latest covers, and the overall message was sex, sex, sex – the more sensational the better. I jotted down three typical coverlines: ARE YOU HOOKED ON SEX? . . . WHAT BOYS LOVE ABOUT BIMBOS (and girls really hate) . . . SEX IN WEIRD PLACES (in the supermarket or on your office desk) . . . Even a new paper, apparently for 11–13-year-olds, was competing: BOYS – WE'VE GOT THEM SUSSED!

Don't be put off yet, because most of this is not nearly as alarming as it may seem at first glance. Those were just coverlines, mere sales gimmicks, making rather desperate grabs for readers. Plunge inside and, apart from a few shock tactics, you'll find plenty of wholesome fun as well as sound advice and comments on careers, leisure activities, health and – need I say it? – relationships.

Writers new to this genre will save themselves time and anguish if they are aware, from the start, of some of the more obvious no-go areas. Not all magazines buy features from freelance writers. Nearly all the articles in one or two younger teenage papers are written by editorial staff, and some editors of young adult journals prefer to commission features from writers known to them, and discourage unsolicited offerings. Fashion, beauty and advice columns are usually written by staff members or regular contributors. A check in the magazines section of this year's edition of one of the writers' yearbooks will give you some of idea of how the land lies.

Original treatment

Earlier in this chapter I mentioned the continuing demand for original ideas, but I'll add here that editors are equally on the lookout for new slants on already popular issues. (Sex *again*? I can almost hear your snorts.) While aspects of relationships remain a high-interest talking-point among teenagers, ingenious writers carry on racking their brains for different angles on what others have rejected as boringly overworked. Subject matter, in some cases, is less important than the manner in which it's presented.

Let's take the well used theme of troublesome flatmates and consider possible ways of attracting new interest. In making it the central issue of an interview feature, for instance, you might introduce three or four young people with experience of this problem, letting them air their differing opinions and ending up with a summary of the more helpful points raised.

Alternatively, you could take a better-safe-than-sorry angle, compiling something along the lines of: 'Choosing a Flatmate – Ten Crucial Tips.'

The subject might be given novelty value when written in the form of a personality quiz. (For example: 'How do you rate as a flatmate?') Editors of magazines for younger teenagers – with most of their readers longing for adult status – might show more interest in a slightly modified approach: 'How *would* you rate as a flatmate?'

Interview features

All editors recognize the attraction of 'big name' interview features as a way of promoting sales. In teenage magazines, the personalities under scrutiny are as often as not pop idols and young stars from the world of entertainment, sport and fashion. Celebrity interviews of this kind are almost always conducted by specially commisioned journalists, well experienced in the required technique – methods of approach through PR companies, for example, the craft of researching for background information and the tactful handling of sensitive subjects *and* people.

Opportunities for beginners lie more in the writing of interview features such as the one about flatmates suggested above. For these, you first have to choose a theme likely to be of interest to teenagers, and then approach a features editor with your basic idea. (More about this shortly.) The next task involves finding a few young people willing to express their thoughts on the matter. (And you'll probably discover that many of them are only too delighted to take part, intrigued at the thought of appearing in a feature of this kind.)

Your way of finding interviewees depends, of course, on what you're writing about, and journalists tend to make good use of friends who work with young people or have children of a suitable age. If, say, you're thinking in terms of an article about hairdressing as a career, your own bright (and photogenic) young stylist might well be happy to chat to you about the pros and cons of her job, supplying amusing little human-angle snippets as well. You'll add more interest to a career feature if you include a separate, fact-file section with carefully checked information on training, salaries, etc. and details with addresses and phone numbers of organizations such as (in this case) the Hairdressing Training Board.

Quite recently I wrote an article about young voluntary workers, and received valuable and friendly help from members of the societies concerned, The Stroke Association and Age Concern among them. I was not only provided with names of possible interviewees, but also given leaflets containing all the information necessary for a properly rounded feature. (Addresses of head offices and local branches of charitable and other orgnaizations may be obtained from telephone directories and public libraries.) An article of this kind benefits from a sprinkling of warmth and humour, and – unless it is for a local publication – should include interviewees from different parts of the country.

Before beginning this chapter, I enlisted the help of my journalist friend, Alison Legh-Jones, who has written countless interview features for national magazines and newspapers, and also worked for several years in the editorial staff training department of IPC Magazines, lecturing on such subjects as 'Research and Interviewing' and 'Feature-Writing'.

She recommended the use of tape recorders, even by journalists proficient at shorthand – and mentioned a famous politician (better left unnamed) who insisted on setting up his own machine when being interviewed, as possible ammunition against misquotes. Mastering the technique of taping takes practice, of course, and I thought back to my own awkward early attempts at using a handbag-size recorder – pressing the wrong buttons and so on. In the end, I forced my son and other victims to let me experiment on them, which was all very hilarious but solved the problem nicely.

For anyone keen to learn more about interviewing, here are some snippets of advice – based on my talks with Alison. These may also be of help to other non-fiction writers hoping to add credibility to their work by including the comments and opinions of specialists in the fields concerned.

- If possible, fix an interview by telephone, partly because some people can't be bothered to reply to letters, and also because many of them seem to find it harder to say 'no' on the phone. Confirm the appointment in writing if this seems sensible, and make sure they have your own phone number in case they wish to cancel.

- Before setting out for the interview, prepare a list of questions. Know exactly what you want to ask. This lessens the risk of drying up and you'll make a better impression if you're concise and to the point from the word go.

- Dress in a way most likely to make your interviewee feel at ease. Jeans and any old shirt may help to convince teenagers that you're not just another snooping geriatric. If you're seeking comments or advice on your subject from an older professional person, it may pay to look fairly respectable and businesslike yourself.

- Be punctual. If you allow good time for any necessary journey and traffic hold-ups, you won't arrive flustered and out of breath. Don't worry if you feel nervous – most interviewers do, to begin with. Resist accepting the offer of an alcoholic drink which will probably make things worse.

- You'll feel calmer once you've begun. Break the ice with a little general chat, and gradually introduce your questions. At some point, check the spelling of your interviewee's name. Even if you are following a teenage magazine's policy of using

Christian names only, take care to get these right. ('John', for example is sometimes spelt 'Jon'.) Check the ages of young interviewees, too, and whether or not they still live at home. Personal details like these add interest and will be appreciated by your readers, when the time comes.

• Particularly in the case of adult interviewees, ask permission to use their full names. Members of certain counselling organizations (the Samaritans, for example) may insist on remaining anonymous. In some types of features, interviewees' names are changed as a matter of course.

• Don't be worried about asking personal questions, but try to establish some sort of rapport first. On the whole, teenagers love talking about themselves and their problems. The most difficult thing, as often as not, is stopping them.

• Don't worry, either, about sounding stupid. If you don't quite catch on to something they say, ask about it. They'll probably be only too pleased to explain snatches of space-age jargon, and your feature won't ring true unless you have a proper understanding of what they've been trying to get across.

• Before you leave, be sure you have learnt all you need to know, because follow-up phone calls may be treated as a nuisance.

• When writing up your feature, make good use of direct speech (i.e. within quotations marks) so that your readers are clearly aware of whose views you are expressing – but always keep to the style of the magazine you are writing for. Some features editors like you to make comments and observations of your own, while others prefer a more objective approach.

There are a few points I'd like to add from my own experience of interviewing young people. Firstly, teenagers are more likely to respond to an adult-to-adult approach. Before firing questions, make it clear that you have to write a feature and badly need their help. Secondly, when talking to a group of three or four, don't allow one of them to dominate the conversation. With friendly encouragement, shyer members may put forward the very opinions you were hoping to hear. Above all, be courteous enough to show a genuine interest in everything that's said.

Quiz features

The popularity of personality quizzes carries on and on, and readers of all ages – 8 to 80 – are apparently happy to accept character assessments made on the basis of their answers to a set of questions posed by a journalist more likely to have a sense of fun than a degree in advanced psychology. (A fair understanding of human nature is, nevertheless, an advantage.)

Most teenage journals run regular or occasional quizzes, with titles such as, 'Are you a Flirt?' or, 'Are you Lucky in Love – and if not, why not?'. For fear of worrying more sensitive readers, some editors make a point of stressing that these features are designed for amusement only. 'Try our fun quiz . . .' the sub-heading might read.

Sometimes a few more serious notes creep in, and there's no harm in that, provided they're not too piously moralistic. A girl whose answers plainly reveal that she is more a menace than a mere flirt may quite rightly be told to watch her step. When compiling features of this type, never lose sight of the fact that you are writing for adolescents – many of them highly impressionable.

Once you've studied a few quizzes, you'll soon pick up the basic technique, but take note of how layout patterns and scoring systems vary from one publication to another. As always when submitting an idea to a magazine, follow its accepted style and you'll stand more chance of catching the editor's interest. Most importantly, work hard at finding an original theme, because competition among quizwriters is fierce.

Marketing magazine non-fiction

'Submit an idea first' was the advice given by most of the features editors I interviewed, and it was also pointed out that suggestions were frequently turned down simply because they were based on topics already covered in recent issues. A brief outline enables an editor, before giving the go-ahead, to decide whether the proposed piece will be of interest to his or her readers – and saves the writer hours of time researching, putting together and typing out a complete article which, for one reason or another, may prove to be unacceptable.

If you have little or no experience of feature writing, you may find it helpful to follow these general rules, which summarize some of the more important points made earlier in this section.

- Choose a magazine which contains material of the kind you have in mind (nothing *too* similar, of course) and consider how you might tailor a feature of your own to fit in with the general style, length and structure.

- Prepare an outline of your idea (say, two or three paragraphs) and your proposed treatment of the subject – main section headings, possible interviewees, etc. Take trouble to be concise without hiding the natural enthusiasm you feel about your chosen theme.

- Write a short covering letter, mentioning previously published work (if any), and offering to send photocopies if required. Say, too, if you can supply photographs or other illustrations. (If you are a competent photographer, you may like to send just one picture, as an example of your work, but label it carefully and don't be too horrified if you never see it again.) Include background details and professional qualifications only if they are relevant to the subject matter of your piece.

- Send your outline, letter etc. with s.a.e. to the features editor, whose name will probably appear in the magazine. (If it doesn't, phone the editorial office and ask; it's better to approach an editor by name.)

- If you've heard nothing after, say, a couple of weeks, a quick and businesslike telephone query is generally acceptable and may speed up a verdict of 'yes' or 'no'. By this time, if you're anything like me, you'll probably feel that anything is better than the awful suffering of uncertainty.

- Feel encouraged if an editor expresses an interest in your idea, and asks to see the completed article. Write it up as quickly as you can, before she loses interest, paying careful attention to any suggestions he or she might have made.

- Follow the general advice given in Chater Three about submitting work to editors: double spacing, clear, clean copy and all the rest of it. Be prepared for a fairly long wait.

Fillers and other exceptions to the 'query-first' rule

In some magazines you'll occasionally find short-short features (of 200 words, say, or maybe even less). They may contain handy hints, money-saving tips, quirky jokes, brainteasers – you name it – and are often used by editors when, for instance, a story runs half a column shorter than expected. If you have an idea which might fit in, covering less than a page of double-spaced typescript, by all means submit it in full. Where time's concerned, you have little to lose and – if it happens to arrive just when something of this kind is needed, you may earn yourself a small fee and possibly even a request for more ideas.

Some how-to-write manuals make mention of the possibility of earning a regular (but very small) income from items published in 'Letters to the Editor' pages but, in the case of teenage magazines, I'm not altogether happy about this idea. Not only does it seem mildly unprofessional, but I also remember working as part of an editorial team and taking my turn to sort through young readers' mail. Most of the letters from older people pretending to be adolescents were instantly recognizable, simply because they didn't ring true, and were rejected for that same reason.

On becoming a regular contributor

Once you have sold an article to a magazine, it makes sense to submit more ideas to the features editor who accepted it, in the hope of establishing yourself as a regular contributor.

Take trouble to build up your reputation as a reliable writer of interesting, well-presented copy, and you may be agreebly suprised, one day, when the editor approaches you, commissioning a feature or asking, even, for suggestions for an entire series.

As a 'regular', you'll gain confidence in yourself and your writing, and enjoy more friendly contact with editorial staff. You may even be encouraged to submit ideas by phone, and will seldom be expected to wait weeks for a verdict. Here are a few points to bear in mind when trying to maintain a good, working, editor-writer relationship.

- When given a deadline, stick to it if humanly possible. If you suspect you won't be able to complete the work in time, say so right from the start. (It's amazing, though, what you can do, under pressure, so don't underestimate your capabilities.

- Don't let your disappointment show or argue too hotly when ideas are turned down. With a little revision, they may be accepted by other magazines.

- Even if you and your editor become good friends, remember that she or he has the final word on editorial policy, so take any criticism to heart and fit in with her suggestions – and even her whims – as best you can. If she loves exclamation marks and you hate them, slot in one or two just to show willing.

- Once established, you may find yourself less careful about presentation, but try not to hand in messy copy, splodged with ballpoint alterations. Retype or reprint where necessary. (If, on the other hand, you've been asked to produce a thousand words overnight, that's a very different matter.)

On this optimistic note, I'd like to end up with a story of my own, which illustrates the value of keeping ears and eyes open for new ideas, wherever you are, whatever you're doing.

About a year ago, a semi-friend invited himself for a meal and, after arriving with a bunch of wilting tulips, spent the entire evening eating my food, drinking my booze and dolling out non-stop advice on my work (he doesn't write), my children (he hardly knows them) and my dodgy financial state (which I prefer not to talk about).

Suddenly, an idea for a feature title flashed through my mind – I swear I actually *saw* it, in capital letters – and I made a grab for a scrap-pad, pretending I wanted to make a note of something he was prattling on about. The very next day, after interesting an editor, Lorna Read, in the feature, I typed it out . . . 'Beware this Man – the Knowall!'

It should have been enough that I actually got paid for airing by grievances, but the story doesn't end there. A month later, Lorna invited me to write a whole series of 1,000-word 'Beware this Man' pieces. True, the theme had a slightly sexist feel about it, but that was the least of my worries. There followed 'The Bully', 'The Mummy's Boy',

'The Holiday Romeo', and so on. (Lorna had ideas of her own about 'The Lecher' and wrote that one herself.)

The moral of this rather smug tale is: capitalize on everything that falls into your lap – even your boring semi-friends.

6
Drama: for stage, radio and television

When working on a novel or short stories, you may find yourself making more and more use of dialogue – as a way of progressing the plot, bringing the characters to life, or simply because you enjoy writing dialogue. If so, you have probably already had some thoughts about writing a play.

It may be that you simply want a change from whatever else you've been working on, and this was certainly the case with Nick Fisher, whose book, *Boys about Boys*, I mentioned on page 71, and who now writes television scripts for both young people and adults. 'I felt I was in danger of being typecast – pigeon-holed as a teenage agony uncle,' he said, pointing out the advantages of showing versatility in the tough, changing world of publishing today.

'At first, no one took my efforts seriously,' Nick went on. 'It took over eighteen months of hard slog – trial scripts, rewrites and encouragement from established playwrights at drama courses – before I made any significant headway.'

And how did he adjust to writing in dialogue? 'That was the least of my problems . . . the pleasurable bit . . . the icing on the cake,' he replied at once. 'The planning is the hard part – hour after hour of structuring and re-thinking.'

Dramatist Steve Gooch clearly shares Nick's view, as you'll see in this extract from the introduction of his book, *Writing a Play*:

> For many people with an inclination towards playwriting, the dialogue – once you're sure of your material – is probably the easiest part. Dialogue seems to flow of its own accord – sometimes too easily – and represents the free, improvisational flow of the writer's imagination. It's the thinking time which is the most difficult to use productively . . .

Anyone wishing to write a play – for stage, television or radio will be helped enormously by a genuine love of drama and the theatre. Much can be learned about technique from a seat in the upper circle, or an armchair in your own living-room, even. And if you can watch or listen to plays in the company of young people – noting their comments and preferences – so much the better. This way you'll learn a lot about the changing demands of older children who are already enjoying adult drama.

We've all read of famous dramatists who were passionately interested in the theatre. When they weren't writing plays, so we're told, they were acting, producing, stage-managing – taking part. (I can't quite resist making mention of William Shakespeare at this point; he's such a heaven-sent example.)

Fanciful talk of Elizabethan actor-playwrights may sound ludicrously out of place to would-be writers of youth drama in the Nineties, but there is still much to be said for practical participation. Roy Apps, author of countless television and radio plays for older schoolchildren, suggested involvement with an amateur dramatic society as one way of gaining first-hand experience of all that goes into the presenting of a play to an audience – from scripting to acting and producing.

Some people seem to be born dramatists and never show quite the same devotion to any other branch of writing. Take the case of Sally Worboyes, now a successful playwright, whose sound advice and enthusiasm I've found invaluable while preparing this chapter . . .

> My love affair with drama began at junior school. We lived in a block of flats in the East End of London, and I remember scribbling plays for the other kids to act. Our stage was one of the landings, and the audience would sit on the stairs . . . It was all I wanted to do . . .

Sally left school at 14 and progressed from typing jobs to a course at the City Lit. ('I suddenly realised I was semiliterate,' she admitted wryly. 'But why wasn't creative writing taught in schools?') When taking part in writers' workshops, she was encouraged by tutors and later gained more practical experience as Residential Writer for the Norfolk Young People's Theatre. She is now in her forties with many radio plays behind her, and is currently working on scripts for popular television series, dividing her time between writing plays – some of them for young audiences – and running courses for writers, new and experienced, at Fen Farm in the glorious wilds of Norfolk (see page 111).

Polly Thomas is another playwright with a keen interest in youth drama – having worked on educational projects here and abroad. (In Paris in the Eighties, she adapted *Othello* for French and English secondary schoolchildren.) Nowadays, she is a director of the New Playwrights Trust in London, a national research and development organization concerned with all forms of live and recorded performance. Membership is open to writers, producers and any other people with interests in new writing.

I strongly recommend the NPT to anyone who has begun, or is seriously considering, writing a play, as another way of becoming personally involved in the world of drama. Members from all over the country receive quarterly bulletins, with news of markets for playwrights, courses, competitions, workshops and events. They also have the use of script and reference libraries, and may take part in the monthly script forum (a rehearsed workshop with professional teams). The reasonably priced script-reading service would, I feel, be of particular value to unestablished writers anxious for advice on their work before submitting it to publishers and producers. 'And', as Polly stressed on our first meeting, 'we have a stated interest in work for young people.'

Adaptations

I spoke to both Polly Thomas and Sally Worboyes about openings for writers considering the idea of adapting existing teenage novels or stories for stage, television or radio, and they both agreed that there was a fair demand for good adaptations. Sally reported that some of her students had shown a keen interest in a recent radio and television drama course on this subject (more about courses in Chapter Seven) and Polly suggested that writers should look for works which were not already widely known.

While mulling over the idea, you'll probably find it useful, and highly enjoyable, to watch or listen to a serialized novel, comparing the dramatized version with the original and noting the scriptwriter's cuts, changes and treatment of the plot and characters as the story unfolds.

If you have a particular book in mind – one which you yourself enjoyed as a teenager, maybe – you should first pay careful attention to the question of copyright. If the author is still alive, you will need his or her permission to work on an adaptation. The publishers of the book will probably be able to put you in contact. As a general rule writers (or their heirs) retain copyright of their works until fifty years after death.

Members of the Society of Authors or the Writers' Guild (see page 109) should seek advice from these organizations if they have any doubts about copyright. If a theatre or broadcasting company has shown interest in your idea, they may be able to help you in your investigations. To avoid disappointment after long hours of work, be sure from the very beginning that you have a right to adapt your chosen book or story.

Programming your mind to drama

Before moving on to the question of specific markets, I'd like to express a few thoughts about playwriting in general. We are, of course, still very much on the subject of fiction, and I hope you'll find help from the first four chapters of this book while pondering over possible themes, plot-construction and characterisation, along with all the nitty-gritty of beginnings, middles and endings. (The sections on dialogue, page 38, and photostory writing, page 64, may be of particular interest.)

While tuning into the idea of writing a play for young people, bear in mind these few basic points:

- From the start, concentrate on *telling a good story* which unfolds naturally – almost, but not entirely, through dialogue. To help you on your way, prepare a scenario (scene-by-scene outline), and use this as a working guide.

- Create your characters as you devise your plot, making sure each of the main ones is necessary to the story itself. Try to hear them talking to you and bring out their individual personalities in the way they speak. As you progress, it will help to read your script out loud from time to time, tape-recording it for further consideration.

- Give plenty of thought to the rhythm of your play. From the first few lines spoken, members of the audience must feel that this is something they'll enjoy. Keep a hold on their interest as you build up the suspense, interweaving episodes of high excitement with snatches of fun, anxiety, despair. Spring surprises now and again, and let human error play its part.

- Round off the story with an ending which neither baffles nor fizzles out weakly. Leave your young audience with something to remember – to talk, think or laugh about afterwards.

STAGE PLAYS

Personal letters and charity work apart, I am, on the whole, against the idea of writing anything without some hope of financial reward, but I have to admit that my own and thousands of other first stage plays were written for love, not money. I clearly remember writing mine during school study periods and it was acted by my classmates at the end-of-term concert. I did it purely for fun, then, little knowing that it would lead (very indirectly) to my being invited to write one of a series of half-hour television plays, targeted at older schoolchildren and any adults who happened to be at home in the late afternoon.

I discussed the question of plots and story lines with actor, Michael Brazier, who spent three years directing youth theatre productions. 'Of course a good story is all-important,' he said, 'but writers should pay just as much attention to the characters as they do to their basic theme.'

Michael also stressed the value to a playwright of hearing (and recording) his or her work read aloud – by a few young family members and friends, perhaps. This is one way of bringing the play to life, assessing good points and bad in both dialogue and structure.

Possible markets

Amanda Smith, editorial director of drama publishers, Samuel French Ltd. (52 Fitzroy Street, London W1P 6JR), supported my view that many playwrights began their careers by writing plays for amateur performances. It's quite usual, for instance, for schoolteachers to submit plays originally written for their own pupils, in the hope of having them published in the form of 'acting editions' for schools and young people's drama groups. The encouraging news is that there is a market for material of the right kind, and these shortened extracts from French's pamphlet of Plays for Youth Theatres will give you some idea of current interests – including the trend, these days, towards multicultural casts. Bear in mind, that plays written for young (unpaid) actors in schools or youth drama groups often have large casts, enabling as many young players as possible to take part. A theatre play for professional actors (paid) is likely to have far fewer characters.

> *Zigger Zagger* by Peter Terson – Specially written for the National Youth Theatre, this play depicts the story of Harry, a football hooligan and his Mephistophelian friend Zigger Zagger. As well as being a picture of contemporary urban society it is also exhilarating theatre.
> CAST: M34, F5. Extras (doubling possible). SCENE: composite setting.

> *You, Me and Mrs Jones* by Tony Horitz – A fast-moving comedy about two unemployed teenagers, uncertain of themselves and the world around them.
> CAST: M10, F9 (doubling possible). SCENE: simple settings.

> *Lords of Creations* by John Wiles. This exciting and fast-moving play is written for a multi-ethnic cast and takes the form of a Balinese folk-tale. There is plenty of scope for the cast to make their own accompanying oriental music.
> CAST: 75 parts (doubling possible). SCENE: A jungle clearing.

You'll find names and addresses of other drama publishers listed in the writers' yearbooks, but anyone keen to write for youth theatres – to study the market, meet people involved – should consider the advantages of membership of the National Association of Youth Theatres. Administrator Angela Kelly explained to me that by no means all members were young acting enthusiasts, and suggested that playwrights might well benefit from their advice services, regional listings and resource library of over 200 scripts, videos and cassettes – and from the bi-monthly magazine and bulletins with information on existing and new theatre groups. To learn more, contact NAYT, Unit 1304, The Custard Factory, Digbeth, Birmingham B9 4AA (Tel. 021–608 2111).

If you are young (15 – 25) and live north of the Border, you may be interested in opportunities for beginner playwrights offered by the Scottish Youth Theatre. 'Every year,' according to the brochure, 'a selection of the best scripts by new writers are rehearsed and presented by professional directors with senior acting students from the Royal Scottish Academy of Music in a festival aimed at highlighting the high standards involved.' For more details, write to the Artistic Director, Scottish Youth Theatre, The Old Athenaeum, 179 Buchanan Street, Glasgow, Gl 2JZ (Tel. 041–332 5127).

London Drama is a voluntary association with a keen interest in youth theatre, and publishes a useful booklet entitled *The Drama Directory*. This gives borough-by-borough information on theatre companies (including youth theatres), arts centres and workshops, and is well worth investigating. For details of membership, write to London Drama, Holborn Centre for the Performing Arts, Three Cups Yard, Sandland Street, London WC1R 4PZ (Tel. 071–405 4519).

Don't overlook the possibility of interesting a local theatre in your work. In its 'Theatre Producers' section, *The Writer's Handbook* provides helpful details of theatres nationwide – some with an interest in plays for young people – and states whether unsolicited manuscripts are considered.

Length and layout of stage plays

It's impossible to be precise about the length of a stage play for young adults, but it would seem sensible to aim for a running time of about 1 ¾ – 2 hours. (Bear in mind, always, that it is easier to cut than to add.) A play which is to be one of several at a youth theatre festival may run for only 30 minutes – and it's sensible to seek advice from the organization concerned.

Of course you can time your work by reading it out loud and, with practice, you'll soon find yourself calculating running time from the number of pages typed, length of speeches, action and so on.

Layouts vary, as you'll note in sample scripts in books such as this, but as a general rule scripts should be typed on one side only of A4 paper, with good-size margins. Use single spacing for speeches and double spacing in between, and capitals for names of characters. Only give stage directions when actors' movements and expressions are not obvious from the dialogue. Here's a brief example of my own:

JASON: Why didn't you tell me this before? (Snatches the letter from KATE'S hand and glances at it briefly) What's the matter with you? Don't you care what happens to me?

KATE: Of course I care. Look what I risked, skiving off work – coming here –

JASON: (Thrusts letter back at KATE) I don't have to listen to this. I should've known you were lying – there were enough warning signs. Goodbye . . . (Stomps off)

Scene 2. KATE sits typing at office desk. HUGO walks up to her.

HUGO: Heard from lover-boy yet, Kate? (Smirks)

KATE: What's it to you? (Carries on typing.)

Attach a title sheet/cast list to your script and submit it with a brief covering letter, mentioning any previously published work. You might also include a brief synopsis as a way of attracting initial interest.

There isn't space in a book of this kind to make an in depth exploration of all, or even half, of what goes into the scripting of a stage play. For a more thorough study of technique, I recommend the handbook I mentioned on page 89: *Writing a Play*, by Steve Gooch.

PLAYS FOR TELEVISION AND RADIO

It's obvious from the long waiting-lists for television drama courses that a great number of would-be playwrights are mainly interested in writing for television. This, of course, means fierce competition – yet again.

When I discussed the question of television plays for young adults with Richard Callanan, Executive producer, BBC Children's Drama (BBC Elstree Centre, Clarendon Road, Boreham Wood, Herts, WD6 1JF), he stressed the need for original ideas . . .' We're looking for variety – something quite different from *Grange Hill* and *Byker Grove*.' He said, too, that experience of scripting radio or stage plays would be of help to new writers, who should mention details of any previously published work when submitting plays to him at the above address. (For details and addresses of independent television companies, refer to current copies of writers' yearbooks.)

Several people concerned with youth drama – playwrights Roy Apps, William Ash and Sally Worboyes among them –

pointed out that there were, on the whole, more openings in radio than in television. At this time of writing, there are several Radio 5 drama slots for plays and serials for older children and teenagers, and anyone interested should write with s.a.e. for an up-to-date list of time slots for different age-groups to: Caroline Raphael, Editor – Drama and Features, Children's and Youth Programmes, BBC Radio 5, Broadcasting House, London W1A 1AA. Scripts should be sent to the same address (again with s.a.e.) but Caroline Raphael stressed that although she was looking for promising material, work would not be commissioned from inexperienced writers on the basis of a synopsis or proposal only. If you have a serial in mind, submit a first episode and a detailed synopsis of the rest, hoping at this stage for encouragment to continue, rather than a formal commission. (Please note that plays should be of entertainment value – this is *not* a schools programme.)

A tremendous amount can be learned about the craft of television and radio playwriting for young audiences by watching and listening – but you'll find out even more by attending one of the many drama courses targeted at both new and experienced writers (see page 110). Apart from gaining confidence in yourself and professional advice on the marketing of your play, you will probably be invited to bring work along to the residential courses and given the benefits of group readings and one-to-one talks with the tutor. Always remember, though, that courses of this kind are only as good as their tutors so pay careful attention to the information supplied in brochures and programme sheets before making a firm booking.

You may prefer to attend local evening classes (public libraries can usually supply details) and, in doing so, meet other beginner-playwrights in your own area. Having said that, I think I ought to add that when I spent five days in Norfolk, on a Fen Farm playwriting course, the only other female student just so happened to live half a mile down the road from me in Hammersmith – and we've been close friends ever since.

Many people find help and pleasure from scriptwriters' play-reading and discussion groups (again look for details in libraries – or in local papers). Player Playwrights – president Jack Rosenthal – is London-based and has been recommended to me several times. At weekly meetings in South Kensington, members are given opportunities to hear their plays read out and commented upon by professional actors and producers. To find out more, write to the secretary, Peter Thompson, 9 Hillfield Park, London N10 3QT (Tel: 081–883 0371).

For anyone feeling too much of a raw beginner to attend such groups and courses, there are several good books available, crammed with information on technique and general know-how, and a few of these are discussed in Chapter Seven, beginning on page 114.

Sally Worboyes' experience of both tutoring and television and radio-playwriting is far greater than mine, so I was delighted when she gave me permission to quote extracts from her article written for *At East* magazine, which now forms part of a set of guidelines used by students at Fen Farm writing courses.

Firstly, here are some of her notes on television playwriting (and the sample television and radio scripts are Sally's, too) . . .

- . . . Choose a time when you can be alone with a note-pad to see how a play or series episode is constructed. Count the number of scenes and exterior actions . . . Count the characters . . . Follow the main character and see in how many scenes he or she appears. If there are any flashback scenes, ask yourself why the writer has chosen that device – would it have worked another way?

- Try not to start writing a play until you have more or less sorted it out in your head. Don't begin a scene until you have the shape of it. Make sure each scene is working towards the point you wish to get to. Use place, time and characters in the piece to convey suspense, intrigue, atmosphere. Every line, every scene, should be driving the action forward while allowing the viewers to discover more and more about the people you wish them to meet: their goals and desires, disappointments and determination. All the stuff of life, with the boring bits left out.

- If, somewhere along the line, you become bored with what you are writing, you may assume that the script-editor will feel the same way when reading it. Stop writing, have a cup of tea, and then return to it . . .

- Keep taking stock as your plays builds. Be faithful to your main character. Make sure he/she remains the main focus of attention. Don't leave her in the laundry because a secondary character grew more interesting. If this happens, maybe the secondary person should *be* your main character. If so, go back to the beginning and change things accordingly.

- One of the questions that nearly always comes up at Fen

Farm is timing. How can we tell how long it is? Try running it through in your head and be the camera when necessary. Roughly speaking, a page typed on A4 paper is about 30 seconds playing time . . .

• Make each character believable – take them from life (and what an assortment we have to choose from) and then make them a tiny bit larger than life. Mix'n match, that sort of thing . . .

• . . . most important – *the story*. Don't rush this part, take it slowly and enjoy it; for this is a time of plotting, contriving, fantasising, creating, dreaming the real and unreal; this is the time when you can put your feet up and tell yourself a story with the wonderful excuse that you are working . . .

SAMPLE SCRIPT. TELEVISION.

EXT. LONDON. BRIXTON. MAIN STREET. MORNING.

A QUEUE HAS FORMED OUTSIDE A PUBLIC BUILDING.

AN ELDERLY WOMAN TAPS IMPATIENTLY ON THE BUREAU WINDOW.

ELDERLY WOMAN: They're in there you know. I just saw one go in the back door.

(TO PATSY) They've threatened to cut my electricity off. That Sharon's good. She'll sort me out. Not keen on Maitrose. Hope I don't get her.

PATSY DOESN'T WANT TO GET INVOLVED IN A CONVERSATION. SHE CHECKS HER SMALL CHILD IN THE PUSHCHAIR, WHO IS FAST ASLEEP.

What's your problem then ?

PATSY REALLY DOESN'T WANT TO DISCUSS HER PROBLEM OR LISTEN TO ANYONE ELSE'S. SHE TUCKS THE BABY'S BLANKET IN.

(TO HERSELF) Suit yerself.

On radio plays Sally Worboyes writes:

• Much of what I have written (about television applies – except, of course, for visuals. You are going to have to get across atmosphere with sound effects.

• You have to push the action forward with dialogue. You must avoid description for description's sake . . . If your character wears flamboyant clothes, we should learn this by the way he or she behaves and by the reaction of other people in the play. If you have a 16-year-old who shops in Oxfam, this tells us something about her. If you have an 80-year-old who shops in Laura Ashley – this gives us an idea of *her* character.

- Use equipment to get across a character's profession/trade. A typewriter, a conveyor belt, a cash register, a milk-cart and so on. Use transport to convey wealth (or lack of it). The Undergound, British Rail, a bike, a car, a bus, aeroplanes. Maybe your character has to walk everywhere ..?

- . . . never make life easy for your players. If they get into a tight spot, you as the author should not get them out of it – that would be lazy. Make *them* find a way round it and you will have a more exciting play.

NIGHT RUNNERS' - A RADIO PLAY TO INTEREST YOUNG ADULTS.

SCENE ONE. NIGHT RUNNERS' - AUTUMN - 1993. EARLY HOURS OF THE MORNING. EXT: FADE UP TO SOUND OF CANAL.

SCENE TWO. INT. MIX TO SOUND OF YOUNG PEOPLE IN DISUSED CANAL SYSTEM - THEIR MAKE-SHIFT HOME.
THEY ARE SLEEPING, SOME TOSSING AND TURNING.

THE LOOK-OUT, GRIFFIN, ARRIVES AND SHAKES THE PACK LEADER, ROACH. HE IS INSTANTLY ALERT.

GRIFFIN (LOW URGENT WHISPER) Turner's outside. He wants to see you. Says it's urgent.

ROACH (SIGHS) All right. Give me a minute. Don't let him in.

GRIFFIN You got it.

SCENE THREE. EXT. SOUND OF CANAL IN BACKGROUND.

TURNER IS USING BODY-MOVEMENTS IN ORDER TO KEEP WARM.
ROACH ARRIVES.

ROACH Turner ?

TURNER We have to talk.

ROACH Yeah ? Well not on my territory, man.

TURNER Do me a favour, Roach. You need a brain-job if you still think we want disused sewer pipes to lay down our bed-roll.
Our warehouse's the place - and you know it.

ROACH You saying we should go there ?

TURNER No way, man. Down by the Canal - mutual ground. Smoke ?

ROACH Yeah... thanks. I'll get a couple of cans; stay right there; don't move an inch, right ?

TUNER Hey... you're preaching to the initiated.

ROACH (APOLOGISING) Nerves are a bit raw.

TURNER Every reason to be. We've got **big problems.**
They're gonna pick us off man; one by one.
The pressure's on - for **clean** streets.

SCENE FOUR: BY THE CANAL. NIGHT.

BOTH ROACH AND TURNER SKIM STONES ACROSS THE WATER.

TURNER You have to believe it, Roach. Four of ours have had severe gut pains; one of which is now extinct.
I'm telling you, man... this is serious.
Spiking remains of fast food ?
Next thing you know they'll bring the firing squad in.

ROACH Anyone else know about this ?

TURNER Stoke Newington and Hammersmith... that I know of. You must have heard... ?

ROACH Course I've heard ! Just needed to hear a bit more...

Okay. We'll converge. (JOVIAL) My place or yours ?

TURNER No way, man. No way.

ROACH You can't hang on to prime territory for ever you know.

7
On becoming a professional

In this chapter I've gathered together a medley of information and books which you may find useful at some stage of your career as a writer for young people . . . beginning with some very basic advice on the likes of grammar and word processors, and progressing to legal matters and Public Lending Right, associations for authors and playwrights, writers' courses, writers' circles.

Grammar and punctuation

Please skip this section if you are a professor of English language. I'm writing it for anyone who's suffering from a surfeit of rejection slips, but may not realize that faulty grammar and spelling could well be part of the problem.

Respectable publishers expect authors to have a good command of their own language; naturally they hope teachers, parents and literary critics will approve of their books for young adults, *and* they want these books to set a good example to the readers themselves.

Most magazine editors feel the same way, and in these days of staff cuts, they can no longer depend on crews of willing sub-editors to spot errors, correct and re-write. One glaring, first-paragraph mistake 'the cat sat on it's mat', for instance, could result in the dumping of a manuscript into the rejection tray.

Whether or not I'm succeeding, I'm trying hard not to sound pompous about all this. Matters of grammar and spelling were mentioned by practically every publisher and editor I interviewed, and this message came across loud and clear: If you want to sell your work, pay attention to the basic rules of good English.

If you suspect there may be serious gaps in your own knowledge, but haven't the inclination or time to attend further education courses, brush up your understanding of the language with a few good books on the subject. Here are three of my own favourites but local librarians and teacher friends will have many more to suggest.

An Introduction to English Grammar by Sidney Greenbaum (Longman). This book is a something of a course in itself – on sentence construction, punctation, spelling and much, much more – and begins rather comfortingly, I think, with an answer to the question: 'What is grammar?' Crammed with easily understood examples of good and bad usage, it also includes a section of exercises, enabling readers to test themselves on their chapter-by-chapter progress. (Furthermore, the author is one of the aforementioned professors of English Language!)

Mind the Stop – a Brief Guide to Punctation by G.V. Carey (Penguin Reference). A delightfully readable and informative little paperback which, according to the *Times Educational Supplement* '. . . presents in a fresh and entertaining way material that might easily have been treated pedantically.' Not so much a rule-book, more a series of discussions, it explains the purpose of each punctuation mark in turn and how and when it should and should not be used. In Chapter Three the author claims that it would be almost true to say 'Take care of the commas and the other stops will take care of themselves . . .' Not altogether seriously, I should perhaps add that when I gave a copy to a journalist friend, for her birthday or something, she was mildly insulted, saying she'd learned all there was to know about punctuation by the age of ten. Did anyone know that much? I wondered (apart, of course, from the late G.V. Carey).

Grammar and Style by Michael Dummett (Duckworth) is the recently published work of yet another university professor. It was written mainly to help students whose examination papers were flawed by glaring mistakes in grammar, punctuation, spelling etc., but I feel it would be equally appreciated by aspiring writers who suspect that their progress is being hampered by an inadequate grasp of the English language. Common faults are pointed out; grammatical principles – subjunctives, transitive and intransitive verbs, split infinitives – are explained and discussed. Very importantly, few serious writers would disagree with this author's claim that: 'Those who trade in the printed word have a duty to the language, over whose use they have an exceptional influence.'

Bloomsbury Good Word Guide, edited by Martin H. Manser, is another useful paperback, giving, as the coverlines rightly state, 'Clear, accessible information and practical guidance on topics as varied as spelling, punctuation, grammar, pronunciation and buzz words . . .' It might also be described as a dictionary of words and terms which are frequently misused, misunderstood and misspelt. Examples of correct usage are given when necessary, for instance, '*Compare to* is used when things are being likened to each other: *He compared her skin to ivory . . . Compare with* is used when things are being considered from the point of view of both similarities and differences: *Tourists find London hotels expensive compared with those of other European captitals*.' The word 'separate' is included simply because it is so often wrongly spelt with an 'e' instead of the first 'a'. There are several excellent books of its kind, but this one would seem to be of particular interest to writers for teenagers, who need, more than most people, to have an understanding of many of the new and sometimes quirky words and expressions constantly creeping into our everyday vocabulary.

Spelling and style

When I was a small schoolgirl, I discovered that 'good spellers' were usually people who were able to see words in their minds in print. I think now that this is an ability we either have or have not, and it's just a matter of luck. If you know you are a 'poor speller', don't worry too much because this needn't stop you from becoming a respected writer, but do consult a dictionary whenever you feel even slightly uncertain. If a member of your family happens to be a wizard at spelling, ask her or him to skim through your work before you submit it. Many word processors have spell-check facilities, but I, for one, still prefer dictionaries. (See page 112)

Throughout this book I've talked about style and how it develops and improves with practice, but there are a few points which, according to writing tutor friends, can't be stressed too often, however elementary they may seem.

• When trying to develop a friendly style, be careful never to sound twee. Just as teenagers resent writers who talk down to them, they've no time either for the kind of exaggerated chumminess sometimes enjoyed by younger children. Enid Blyton loved turning sentences into questions, 'That was a silly thing to do, wasn't it?', which was fine for the under-sevens, but too cloying by half for anyone else. By all means try to involve your readers, but don't put them off by going way over the top.

• Try to avoid using the same word too often. For example instead of writing, 'We had a great time on the beach and the party afterwards was great . . .' you might put, 'We had a great time on the beach and the party afterwards was amazing . . .' (Or 'brilliant' or 'supersonic' or whatever newer expression takes your fancy – anything but a repeat of 'great'.) Avoid also the overuse of adjectives. Ask yourself if they're actually needed.

• Whenever possible, create an original expression of your own instead of resorting to a cliché (e.g. the likes of 'raining cats and dogs' or 'wolf in sheep's clothing'). When I worked on a teenage fiction magazine, editors and subs used to cringe at one particularly overworked sentence, 'We got on so well it was as if we'd known each other all our lives.' True, there was nothing downright sinful about this, but it seemed to appear, in various guises, on every other unsolicited manuscript we read.

Choosing word-processing equipment

Some people call them word processors, others talk of PCWs (Personal Computer Word processors), and since beginning work on this book, I've prayed nightly that mine wouldn't break down before the sinister deadline.

If you asked me whether they're worth the expense involved, I'd say YES, in block capitals – provided you've a serious interest in writing to sell. Suddenly, editing and the correction of errors become a doddle, the retyping of messy-looking pages is a thing of the past, and professional presentation is possible with the minumum of effort. If you are as ignorant about computers as I was before buying mine, here are a few suggestions to help you on your way.

• Enlist the patient assistance of a computer-minded friend before and after buying your word processor. Better still, if you know the owner of one, ask if you may try it out.

• Don't let some electronic whizz-kid persuade you to buy a far more sophisticated machine than you need as a writer, but if you intend to write a book, consider the optional extra of a double disk drive. With this you will be able to safeguard each day's work by copying it on to a back-up disk in a matter of seconds instead of minutes.

• Pay careful attention to the matter of printers. Ask for demonstrations and bear in mind that, for good presentation, you'll need a type style of the kind known as 'letter quality' or 'near-letter quality'. Speed, noise and compactness should all be taken into account.

• Instruction manuals are notoriously difficult to follow, but with the help of one of those long-suffering, computer-minded friends, you'll soon get the hang of things. (Courses are sometimes available – ask your dealer about these and helpline information services.)

The writer and the law

When working on teenage magazine, *Loving,* I became increasingly aware of how important it was for writers to have at least a smattering of legal knowledge, and I was lucky enough to be sent on a law course for journalists, conducted by barrister, Peter Mason, legal adviser to IPC Magazines Ltd. Although semi-retired now, he was kind enough to help me with this section. I mention racism first because several publishers have warned me that this was something that writers for young people should be very careful about.

• *Racism:* Under Race Relations Legislation, it is an offence to publish material likely to incite racial hatred or contempt. Be wary, too, of subject matter that might be considered to be offensive on religious grounds.

• *Libel:* Broadly speaking, this means writing about someone alive in such a way as to damage his or her reputation or character in the eyes of reasonable people. One problem area is what lawyers call 'innuendo', i.e. writing something that, because of personal circumstances, becomes a damaging comment – in other words don't insinuate. Libel is a complicated subject, a well-known cause of nightmares and applies to both fiction and non-fiction. Of course novelists slot people they know into their books, but be careful!

- *Plagiarism*: You may also be sued for copying another writer's work without first being granted his or her permission (i.e. infringement of copyright). You could even land yourself in trouble for pinching a novelist's plot, though this might be more difficult to prove. In non-fiction, it is acceptable to quote snippets here and there, but the source of these should always be acknowledged in the text. In general, there is no copyright on ideas; cookery writers 'borrow' each other's recipes all the time, but material should never be copied word for word. When the style and wording are completely changed, there is less cause for concern but, again, be careful! Your publisher may be able to help on all three of these points, because they've no wish to be sued, either.

- *Contracts*: Be absolutely certain you're being offered a fair deal before signing a publisher's contract. If you enlist the help of a solicitor, make certain she or he has specialist knowledge of publishing matters. Both the Society of Authors and the Writers' Guild offer their members contract-vetting services (see opposite) and Michael Legat's handbook, *An Author's Guide to Publishing* has a useful chapter on contracts. (More details on page 48.)

For anyone anxious for an in-depth understanding of contracts, Peter Mason recommended Charles Clark's book, *Publishing Agreements*, published by Butterworth and rather costly, so seek it out at a public library. Among other things, this goes through a sample contract, page by page, explaining in layman's language the wording and effect of each clause.

Ups and downs – Public Lending Right and income tax.

Once you have had a book published, you are legally entitled, as a resident in the UK or Germany, to receive an annual, government-funded payment, based on the number of borrowings from sample public libraries. Although it may not be very much, it's nice when it happens, usually in the bleakness of February or March. You must register the book (and further books) yourself, the sooner after publication day the better, and full details and application forms may be obtained from: The Registrar, PLR Office, Bayheath House, Prince Regent Street, Stockton-on-Tees, Cleveland TS18 1DF (Tel. 0642–604699).

Less cheerfully, I should perhaps remind you that earnings from your writings are subject to Income Tax. Your working expenses, anything from a rubber to a word processor, and much more besides, are tax deductible, so it's wise to keep all receipts safely in a folder. Unless you are a very businesslike person, you'll probably find it pays to seek the advice of an accountant, preferably one with other writers on his books.

ASSOCIATIONS, COURSES AND WRITERS' CIRCLES

Many of the organizations listed in the writers' yearbooks provide ways of meeting other writing people, but the following two highly respected associations also exist to support, advise and protect professional writers at every stage of their careers.

The Society of Authors is an independent trade union, representing writers' interests in all aspects of the writing profession, including publishing, broadcasting, television and films – and there are specialist groups for children's and educational writers. Members receive advice, when needed, on negotiations (including clause-by-clause vetting of contracts) and help in pursuing legal actions for breach of contract, copyright, etc. Full membership is restricted to those authors who have had a full-length work published, broadcast or performed commercially in the United Kingdom – but writers who have had a full-length work accepted for publication but not yet published, or have had short stories or other items published, may apply for associate membership. Further information can be obtained from the Society of Authors, 84 Drayton Gardens, London SW10 9SB (Tel. 071-373 6642).

The Writers' Guild (affiliated to the TUC) provides similar benefits and represents writers' interests in film, radio, television, theatre and publishing. Its basic function is to negotiate minimum terms in those areas in which its members work. Regular social events are held, enabling new members to meet one another and exchange ideas on an informal basis. Membership is based on a points system and full details can be obtained from the Writers' Guild, 430 Edgware Road, London W2 1EH (Tel. 071–723 8074).

Writers' courses

Don't be put put off by the shortage of courses designed specifically for writers of teenage literature. On a novel-writing course, you'll quite likely meet would-be authors of science fiction books, Mills and Boon-style romances and thrillers. They are there to learn about technique, to discuss style and themes – and a variety of aims usually leads to a more interesting time for all involved.

Meeting other writers, some experienced, others near-beginners, is much more than a fringe benefit for anyone who *wants* to meet other writers. If you're a loner then perhaps courses are not for you, and there are other ways of learning techniques.

I've already mentioned the possiblity of evening classes and workshops in your own area and, although your local library may be a good source of information, you will find details of courses, up and down the country from the writers' yearbooks.

Residential courses are becoming more and more popular and some offer chances of group and one-to-one tuition and discussions with established writer-tutors in peaceful rural surroundings. The Arvon Foundation, perhaps the leader in this field, now has centres in Devon, West Yorkshire and the Scottish Highlands. Here are a few extracts from a recent brochure:

> There is no entrance qualification for an Arvon course: the only requirement is a strong desire to write. People of all ages (over sixteen) may be writing seriously for the first time in their lives; others may have been writing for years and already have had work published or performed. . . Arvon provides the opportunity for living and working with established writers in an informal atmosphere. While the writers are called 'tutors', they do not give formal teaching but are here to share their skills and imagination, and give personal advice to each member of the course. . .

As one now published novelist, said, 'I went home feeling there were other people like me. I wasn't some kind of freak, after all – and this gave me the confidence to go on.' For programme details, write to the Arvon Foundation at Totleigh Barton, Sheepwash, Beaworthy, Devon EX21 5NS or

Lumb Bank, Hebden Bridge, West Yorkshire, HX7 6DF or Moniack Mhor, Moniack, Kirkhill, Inverness IV5 7PQ.

I've already mentioned the 5-day courses for writers at Fen Farm in Norfolk, which are run on lines similar to those at Arvon centres. Here students are expected to help themselves to breakfast and lunch from a well-stocked kitchen, dinner is cooked and cleaned away by popular resident chef, Darren. The tutors, often best-selling authors or playwrights, live on the premises and often take part in log-fireside discussions way into the night. Playwright director Sally Worboyes said 'We get lots of children's writers here, and at one television and radio drama course, two of our students were tackling plays for young people. A talented girl brought the first pages of her book for adults to a novel-writing week, but changed direction mid-course after being advised that her work had the makings of a lively teenage romance.' For details of courses, write to Sally Worboyes 10 Angel Hill, Bury St Edmunds, Suffolk IP33 1UZ.

If you insist on a bedroom of your own, prefer to be nearer London or are looking for a shorter break, investigate the courses for writers at Missenden Abbey (linked with Southern Arts), another delightful rural retreat. Students have single study bedrooms, and meals are of superb quality. April Halton, the friendly Head of Residential Adult Education told me of the care taken in the choosing of well-qualified tutors. For details, write to Missenden Abbey Weekends, Great Missenden, Buckinghamshire, HP16, OBD. (Writers' courses are also a feature of the Missenden Abbey Summer School.)

Several enthusiasts drew my attention to the popularity of the Swanwick Writers' Summer School, a week of lectures, tuition sessions, discussion groups and events for new and established writers. Apply early in the year to Mrs Philippa Boland, The Red House, Marsdens Hill, Crowborough, East Sussex TN6 1XN

Writers' circles

Some people rave about them, others shudder at the very idea, but many writers (beginners in particular) thoroughly enjoy these regular get-togethers in their own areas, where members read and comment on each other's work and take part in companionable discussions. I'm told some of the criticism can be brutally frank, so participants need to have fairly thick skins. For a national Directory of Writers' Circles write to editor, Mrs Jill Dick, Oldacre, Horderns, Park Road, Chapel-en-le-Frith, Derbyshire SK12 6SY.

BOOKS AND MAGAZINES FOR WRITERS

This is my personal selection from the baffling array of publications currently available for writers, and I've given my own reasons for including them. I've mentioned the two writers' yearbooks many times, and they are on sale in most bookshops, so I suggest you browse through both before deciding which is more suited to your needs. Lots of people buy a different one each year, which seems quite a sensible idea but it is essential to have an up-to-date copy of one or the other.

Dictionaries and books of general interest

The Concise Oxford Dictionary (Oxford University Press) This is my current favourite, because it's easy to handle and gives brief but helpful notes on correct usage. ('Similar' we are told, is often followed by 'to'.) Whichever dictionary you prefer, make sure you have a fairly up-to-date edition.

Collins A-Z Thesaurus (HarperCollins) Always useful when you're hunting for just the right word, or trying to avoid using the same word twice in one paragraph. To some people, the word 'thesaurus' is synonymous with 'Roget' but I find the A-Z format far easier to cope with.

Gem Dictionary and Thesaurus (HarperCollins) Small enough to be tucked into a pocket or handbag, this is too limited for everyday use, but handy when you're taking work away for a weekend or whatever.

Hutchison Concise Encyclopedic Dictionary (Helicon) I find this invaluable as a combined word and fact-finder. It has entries on people, places, technology, mythology, politics, etc.

Writers' and Artists' Yearbook (A & C Black). A fund of information for writers and artists, with details of book publishers, newspapers, magazines, theatres, associations and so on. There are countless features of general interest, too, and a section on proof-reading symbols.

The Writer's Handbook edited by Barry Turner, (Macmillan) As I've said, some swear by this and others prefer the Yearbook. The information is presented differently, but it's all there and the style is friendly. If you've an interest in playwriting, the drama section is particularly good.

Research for Writers by Ann Hoffmann (A & C Black). Described by Shirley Conran as 'indispensable', this gives sound advice on sources of information for writers of fact and fiction, and includes information on the use of libraries, factual, historical and picture research, indexing and other reference books for writers.

Writing for Pleasure and Profit by Michael Legat (Robert Hale). The author is well known for his handbooks, which provide immensely useful nitty-gritty-type information and advice to writers. This one covers novels, non-fiction books and articles, plays, and writing for children – and gives tips on accurate word counts, presentation and selling. (I've discussed another of Legat's books, *An Author's Guide to Publishing* on page 48)

Word Power by Julian Birkett (A & C Black) A delightfully readable book about creative writing and story-telling, with useful sections on plotting, dialogue and drama. It would make a good present for a writer friend, but enjoy it yourself first.

Becoming a Writer by Dorothea Brande (Macmillan Papermac). Books for writers come and go, but this classic by a teacher of writing – first published in 1934 – lives on. My own copy, now battered and rarely, if ever, lent out, has been a source of inspiration for many years and a comfort when all else fails. In the author's own words, 'This book is about the writer's magic'.

'Best-selling novelist, John Braine, claims in his foreword to a recent edition that it is the *only* book about writing that has been of practical help to him – later adding, 'To me it is much more than a book: it is a wise and loving friend. No writer can do without it . . . It has shown me for the first time what writing is. And it has shown me how a writer must live. And, I hope, grow.'

On novel-writing

The Craft of Novel-Writing by Dianne Doubtfire (Allison & Busby). This was recommended to me by novelist, Stan Barstow, whose claim on the coverlines is: 'I devoured it at once . . . full of good sense and valuable insights.' Furthermore it was almost the only book I found with a whole chapter devoted to the writing of a teenage novel.

Writing Historical Fiction by Rhona Martin (A & C Black). This is a splendidly helpful guide for anyone keen to write a historical novel, but unsure of how to cope with all the research involved. (Most of us wouldn't know where to begin). The author is a prize-winning historical novelist and brings in the observations of other specialists in this field.

On drama and playwriting

Writing a Play by Steve Gooch (A & C Black). I've discussed this book already in Chapter Four, and its value to would-be writers of stage plays.

The Way to Write Radio Drama by William Ash (Elm Tree Books). I met Bill Ash on a Fen Farm course and his teaching skills are evident in this friendly, informative book. It begins with a fascinating history of the radio play, and moves on to discuss themes and plots, construction, characterization, sound effects, dialogue, and much more. There are sample scripts and a useful section on the differences between radio and visual drama.

Writing for Television by Gerald Kelsey (A & C Black). If, in spite of the competition, you're determined to write a television play, this is the handbook for you, and it has a useful section on writing for children, as well as sample scripts, and chapters on exteriors and locations, story construction, dialogue, marketing – and one intriguingly entitled, 'The land of mockbelieve'. The author has contributed scripts to a great many BBC and ITV drama series and for children's programmes, and is a former Chairman of the Writers' Guild.

Plays and Players is a lively magazine for anyone with an interest in the theatre, playwrights for young audiences included. For example, in a recent issue, I noted a full-page feature on drama in schools. 'Theatre is for everyone,' editor

Sandra Rennie claimed. 'At one time our journal might have had a somewhat "elderly lady" image, but we've now given her a face lift – brought her right up to date.' The magazine, which includes sections on television and radio drama, is available from theatre foyers and selected bookstalls. (For further details, telephone: 081–343 8515.)

General interest magazines for writers

You may find these useful with their news of markets, courses, conferences, competitions and events for writers. Features include interviews with authors and publishers, book reviews and articles on various branches of writing and journalism (not a lot about the teenage market). *Writing Magazine* can be bought from bookstands, but some are available by subscription only. The two below occasionally advertise free trail offers, so ask about these if phoning or sending for details. *Writers News* – P.O. Box 4, Nairn IV12 4HU (Tel. 0667–54441) *Writers' Monthly* – 29 Turnpike Lane, London N8 OEP (Tel. 081–342 8879)

Books for teenagers and older children

Books discussed in this and other chapters are listed on page 123. Of possible interest to writers studying the market is the Book Trust's Children's Library, which aims to stock all children's titles (age range 0–16) published within the last two years. (Contact: Ann Sohn-Rethel, Book Trust, Book House, 45 East Hill, London SW18 2QZ Tel: 081–870 9055). The Book Trust Scotland information service has a reference library with all books for this age group published in the last 12 months. (Contact: Lindsey Fraser, The Scottish Book Centre, 137 Dundee Street, Edinburgh EH11 1BG Tel. 031–229 3663)

8
Problems shared

Perhaps the most enjoyable part of writing this book has been the contact I've made with other writers: not just friends and one-time colleagues, but people I'd never met before, who have cheerfully provided information, opinions and support – and they, too, have become friends along the way.

So I'm partly, but not entirely, handing this chapter over to them. Established authors often come up against the same problems and tough decisions faced by beginners, but experience has taught them how to cope. (More or less, I suppose.) So let's consider a few of these hassles, and end with some observations on that recurring disease called Writer's Block.

On changing direction

You may be considering the possibility of a novel or play for teenagers after establishing yourself as a writer for adults or younger children, possibly because your interest has been aroused by the books and magazines left scattered around the house by your growing-up children, or simply because you feel you need a change. If you're at all daunted by the idea of switching from a safe source of income or pleasure to something still bafflingly new, feel heartened by the story of Christine Pullein-Thompson, who decided to tackle a teenage novel after decades of writing pony stories for junior school readers.

Horses and writing were part of Christine's life from early childhood, and her mother, Joanna Cannan, was the writer of pony books during and after the second world war. (She was certainly my own favourite author once long ago.) As schoolgirls, Christine and her sisters, Diana and Josephine, acquired a battered typewriter and wrote pony stories, too. Christine left school aged 14½ and started a riding stables with her sisters, and later went to America as a professional rider, before deciding that writing was 'easier and more profitable'. Nearly seventy pony books after that, she found time to stop and wonder about her successful but, in some ways, single-track career:

> Suddenly, I wanted to be judged on something else. However popular my books, however much I enjoyed writing them, I didn't want to be typecast – as one of those sisters who wrote pony stories. The change in direction wasn't difficult at all – it was rather exhilarating – maybe because I was ready for it.

When Christine came to lunch earlier this year, she brought two of her books. One, *Phantom Horse,* for young riding addicts, was first published in 1955 and is still being reprinted. It begins, as good stories often do, with signs of approaching conflict. Protagonist Jean and her brother Angus – very much 'the children' – are told of their father's new job, which will mean a move to America, 'But what will we do with the ponies? We can't take them. . .'

The other book, *Father Unknown* is a love story, and was first published in the early Eighties, when teenage romances were fast becoming big business for British publishers. In this, too, conflict is present on the very first page, but there the similarity ends. Protagonist Sophie, bloodstained and distraught, is waiting for an ambulance after a scuffle with schoolmates who had taunted and accused her of being a virgin and a lesbian.

Don't feel that change of direction means you may never go back to you good old ways. Before returning to her horses in Suffolk, that day, Christine Pullein-Thompson smiled at me and said:

> Mention my teenage novels in your book if you want to, but don't say I gave up on pony stories altogether. I'm working on an idea for one now . . . I *like* writing them. . .

Kenneth Ireland's change was from adventure thrillers for 10-to-14-year-olds to non-fiction books for the same age group – at a time when there was a lull in the demand for young adult novels. I've already mentioned the success of his *Who Invented, Discovered, Made the First. . .?* and *True*

Ghost Stories. He said he had been encouraged, early on, after being told that publishers of non-fiction often showed keen interest in ideas from established writers of fiction, because 'at least they knew they could write.'

Ken added happily that he still, on the whole, preferred fiction, but had been doing a balancing act, recently writing novels for overseas markets and non-fiction for publishers here in Britain.

Meeting the readers

At the beginning of this book I stressed how important it was to meet and talk to the teenagers you were writing for, and, knowing this was wasn't easy for some people, I mentioned a few of my own ways of keeping in touch, after my daughters and son had grown up. I also described how novelist Pete Johnson had gathered together a panel of readers from all over the country, who reviewed and, if necessary, criticized his work long before it reached a publisher's desk.

This all started some years ago when Pete, who was then a teacher, enlisted the help of some of his pupils, asking them to comment on passages of a story he was working on. When he and I met, I pointed out that not all writers met teenagers as part of their everyday work.

He agreed, but suggested that anyone interested should consider as a start making contact, by letter, with a school librarian, who might be only too willing to organise a writer-and-pupils discussion group. (Staff at public libraries often have links with local schools and may be able to put you in touch.)

Don't feel that young people won't want to talk. Pete and I both find that keen readers are usually happy to be asked for their opinions, and he introduced me to two young people who have been helping him for some time now.

Clare Slack (17) met Pete three years ago, when he visited her school in Derbyshire, and she's still an enthusiastic member of his panel.

> It's fun – I really enjoy being part of it – and apart from anything else, it gave me a serious interest in other books, too. I learned what to look out for, and gained a new understanding of what writers were getting at. I still like Pete's books even now . . .

Darren Rumble (19) met Pete two years ago at a college evening course on film studies . . .

> Of course I was pleased when he asked me to help – it was a new interest and it's helped *me* in lots of ways, too. I didn't know what I wanted to do then, but I'm writing quite a lot myself now. Being on the panel – analyzing and doing a bit of editing here and there – that's what started me off.

In these cases there seems to have been quite a lot of give and take, and everyone benefited.

On writing a book while doing a full-time job

Lots of people don't believe this is possible, until they've tried it for themselves. I discussed the matter with magazine editor and novelist, Lorna Read, and she offered these few guidelines – some more serious than others.

- It won't work unless you discipline yourself. (Well, it certainly doesn't for me, anyway.) When I'm working on a book, friends are banned from my flat, at least four evenings a week.

- Don't set yourself impossible tasks, like 3,000 words a night, or your daytime job will suffer, and so will your book. If you can drag yourself out of bed at six a.m., so much the better.

- Don't base your hero on someone in the office. It could lead to all sorts of trouble – and he might get the wrong idea if he catches you gazing purposefully at him three times in one afternoon.

- If it's humanly possibly, avoid telling colleagues that you're writing the book. On hearing about it, the boss might suspect (rightly or wrongly) that your work for his company was no longer your first priority in life.

- Make good use of your lunch hours for doing necessary research at libraries and elsewhere. While working on your book, make sure you have a Radio Times, or other guide, so that you can video-tape daytime programmes which may help in some way.

Bringing up children can be more than a full-time job, and playwright Sally Worboyes forced herself to observe a 'kids first' rule when hers were very young. As soon as they were old enough for school, she was back at her desk most days. She also started up a young people's drama group in her village, which was fun all round and involved her family in her work.

Novelist Annie Dalton wrote to survive and found life tough as a working mum.

> I remember cycling furiously home from playgroup, to give myself two hours of peaceful writing before returning to collect my youngest child at lunchtime. The other mothers didn't altogether approve of me, because I was the only one who paid a little extra in order to be deleted from the rota of one-morning-a-week helpers. Once the kids were all at proper school, I became absolutely plugged in and their escapades provided plenty of fuel for my stories.

On the question of steam

In Chapter One, I discussed the matter of sexual encounters in teenage books but, realizing this troubles some writers (how much unbridled passion, if any?), I asked novelist Mary Hooper for her views.

> When my children were young teenagers, I would have been highly embarrassed writing anything about sex. My daughter would have been mortified – especially as her friends read my books, too. They are older now, but I'm still not happy about writing about sex for this age group. I just don't think it's on. A recent outline for a new series for 10-to-13-year-olds asked for 'discreet sex, a backdrop to the plot', but I'm afraid that any sex I put in a teenage book would be so discreet as to be unnoticeable: a kiss on the cheek would be about as far as it went.
>
> It's a little different with magazines intended for readers aged 16-plus, although I suspect these are bought and enjoyed by younger children. To save your family terminal embarrassment, I suppose you could ask for your sexy stories to be published under another name!

Writer's block – real or imaginary?

It's the oldest writing joke in the world, beloved of jaded scriptwriters when they, too, have run out of better things to say . . . 'He's in a terrible state – tearing his hair out – yelling at everyone he's got writer's block.' So what's it all about? Most of us have off-days when we sit, bereft of ideas, staring morosely at blank sheets of paper, or screens, which in turn leer back at us from inactive machines. It's a terrifying feeling, one we all dread, and that's why I asked friends in the trade for their thoughts on this indescribably frustrating malady.

No one was much help. Journalist Alison Legh-Jones said the only answer was to keep typing – typing anything – until the right words began to flow again. She added that she usually had to work to deadlines, so it benefited her, when blocked, to remind herself of this. If she didn't produce the goods on time, she didn't get paid. And that was it.

Different writers have different methods of beating the block: walking the dog, phoning a friend, having a bath. One girl found it helped to take on another, deadly boring job, and might even get down on her knees and start cleaning out the fridge; after half an hour of that, she said, the sit-down task of conjuring up inspiration was childsplay.

Still searching for a known cure, or at least a scientific explanation, I phoned psychiatrist friend, Dr David Bennett, who sympathized but didn't altogether agree with people who looked on writer's block as a bona fide disease. He advised them to consider two possible causes for the complaint. The first – unsurprisingly enough, these days – was external stress. The other was sheer exhaustion.

The stress suggestion, I decided, after saying thank you and goodnight, was worth considering. I've often found it difficult to think straight when my mind was more concerned with the pressing need, say, of a 'friendly talk' with the bank manager – or even the irritation of having to rush out and buy something delicious but near-instant from Marks and Spencer for the neighbour, or whoever, I shouldn't have been silly enough to invite for dinner that evening. Problems of this kind have to be dealt with before I can begin to think constructively about an imaginative beginning to Chapter Three. Or Six, or Eight.

As for exhaustion – that seems to make sense, too. If a man regularly works all day at an outside job and spends half the night tussling with his book at home, there may come a time when his brain goes on strike – opts out until it gets its breath back. This could be likened to the way an electronic device (mine for one) reacts when too much data is fed into its memory in the space of too short a time; suddenly it goes haywire and horrendous messages flash across the screen, warning the operator to slow up or risk losing some or all of that precious data.

I want to give the last word to Dorothea Brande, whose book, *Becoming a Writer*, I raved about in Chapter Seven. When discussing 'The Writers's Recreation' she wrote:

> If you want to stimulate yourself into writing, amuse yourself in wordless ways. Instead of going to a theater, hear a symphony orchestra, or go by yourself to a museum; go alone for long walks, or ride by yourself on a bus-top. If you will conscientiously refuse to talk or read you will find yourself compensating for it to your great advantage.

Translating that advice into terms relevant to present-day writers for young adults, I'd say: when you're lost for words, take a short break. Find yourself a few minutes' breathing space in a place where teenagers are neither seen *nor* heard.

Book list

Fiction

Adler, Sue, (ed.), *Mightier than the Lipstick* Puffin Books 1992
Buchan, John, *The Thirty-Nine Steps* Penguin 1991
Chambers, Aidan (ed.), *A Sporting Chance* Macmillan 1988
Coburn, Ann, *The Granite Beast* Bodley Head 1991
Cormier, Robert, *I am the Cheese* Collins Tracks, HarperCollins 1979
    The Chocolate War Collins Tracks, HarperCollins 1987
Dalton, Annie, *Naming the Dark* Methuen 1992
Daly, Maureen, *Seventeenth Summer* Holis and Carter
Doherty, Berlie, *Dear Nobody* Hamish Hamilton 1991
Fine, Anne, *The Book of the Banshee* Hamish Hamilton 1991
    Goggle-eyes Hamish Hamilton 1989
    Taking the Devil's Advice Penguin 1991
Garner, Alan, *The Owl Service* Collins 1981
Gatti, Will, *Absolute Trust* Pan 1991
Golding, William, *Lord of the Flies* Faber & Faber 1954
Hardcastle, Michael, *Penalty* Dent 1991
Harris, Jesse, *The Power* (series) Red Fox 1993
Hodgson, Miriam, (ed.) *Take your Knee of my Heart* Mammoth 1990
Hooper, Mary, *Making Waves* Methuen (reprint in preparation)
Horowitz, Anthony, *Groosham Grange* Methuen 1988
Ireland, Kenneth, *A Ghostly Gathering* Hodder & Stoughton 1992
Johnson, Pete, *We, the Haunted* HarperCollins 1989
    One Step Beyond Mammoth 1990
Laird, Elizabeth, *Kiss the Dust* Heinemann 1991
Lingard, Joan, *The Twelfth of July* Penguin 1989
Margorian, Michelle, *A Little Love Song* Methuen 1991
McAfee, Annalena, *The Girl Who Got to No. 1* Julia McRae 1991
Orwell, George, *Animal Farm* Penguin 1989
Pascal, Francine, *Sweet Valley High* (series) Bantam
Pullein-Thompson, Christine, *Phantom Horse* Ravette 1989
    Father Unknown Dobson 1982
Pullman, Philip, *The Tiger in the Well* Viking 1991

Read, Lorna, *City Sax* Virago 1988
Salinger, J.D., *The Catcher in the Rye* Penguin 1969
Scott, Hugh, *The Haunted Sand* Walker 1991
Shaw, Bob, *Killer Planet* Gollancz 1989
Sheringham, Sally, *Cuckoo in the Nest* Hodder & Stoughton 1991
Stones, Rosemary, *Loving Encounters* Picadilly 1988
Swindells, Robert, *Stone Cold* Hamish Hamilton 1993
Tolkien, J.R.R., *The Lord of the Rings* Grafton, HarperCollins 1991
Townsend, Sue, *The Queen and I* Methuen 1992
Ure, Jean, *Plague 99* Mammoth 1991
A Place to Scream Doubleday 1992
Westall, Robert, *Ghost Abbey* Hippo 1988
A Walk on the Wild Side Methuen 1989
Zindel, Paul, *The Pigman* Bodley Head 1993

Non-fiction

Ash, William, *The Way to Write Radio Drama* Hamish Hamilton 1985
Bawden, Juliet, *Zany Jewellery* Magnet
Birkett, Julian, *Word Power* A & C Black 1993
Blume, Judy, *Letters to Judy* Pan Books 1987
Brande, Dorothea, *Becoming a Writer* Macmillan 1983
Carey, G.V., *Mind the Stop* Penguin 1971
Clark, Charles, *Publishing Agreements* Butterworths 1993
Corey, Peter, & May, Kara, *Coping with Girls/Coping with Boys* Hippo Books 1992
Dawson, Jill, *How do I Look?* Virago 1991
Doubtfire, Dianne, *The Craft of Novel-Writing* Allison & Busby 1981
Drummett, Michael, *Grammar and Style* Duckworth 1993
Farman, John, *The Very Bloody History of Britain* Red Fox 1992
Fisher, Nick, *Boys about Boys* Piccadilly Press 1991
Gooch, Steve, *Writing a Play* A & C Black 1988
Greenbaum, Sidney, *An Introduction to English Grammar* Longman 1991
Hoffmann, Ann, *Research for Writers* A & C Black 1992
Ireland, Kenneth, *True Ghost Stories* Hippo Books 1989
Unsolved Mysteries Hippo books 1988
Who Invented the First? Ravette 1993
Book of Discoveries Ravette 1993
Kelsey, Gerald, *Writing for Television* A & C Black 1990
Legat, Michael, *An Author's guide to Publishing* Hale 1991
Writing for Pleasure and Profit Hale 1986
Manser, Martin, H. (ed.), *Good Word Guide* Bloomsbury 1990
Martin, Rhona, *Writing Historical Fiction* A & C Black 1988

Pain, Helen, *Where to Join?* Northcote House 1988
Sharpe, Sue, *Know Your Rights* HarperCollins 1991
Wade, R.G., & Nottingham, Ted, *Check out Chess* Puffin 1989
Wells, Gordon, *Magazine Writer's Handbook 1993/4* Allison & Busby 1992
Wheatley, Nadia (ed.), *Landmarks* Turton & Chambers 1991

Other general reference books mentioned in the text:

Collins A–Z Thesaurus, HarperCollins
Concise Oxford Dictionary, Oxford University Press
Hutchinson Concise Encyclopedic Dictionary, Helicon
Writers' and Artists' Yearbook, A & C Black
Writer's Handbook (ed. Barry Turner), Macmillan

Index